EDIBLE AND MEDICINAL WILD PLANTS OF BRITAIN AND IRELAND

ROBIN HARFORD

Eatweeds
47 Old Abbey Court,
Salmon Pool Lane,
Exeter, EX1 2DS
United Kingdom

eatweeds.co.uk

CONTENTS

FREE PHOTO IDENTIFICATION GUIDE

Most wild flower books only provide one photo of each plant for identification. Then a little bit of botanical description. Usually using words that don't mean anything to anybody, unless you are a botany geek.

To forage plants safely, you need a specialist plant identification guide. Which is why in this book there are no pictures, nor a botanical profile.

Instead I have created a FREE *Photo Identification Guide to Edible and Medicinal Wild Plants* for you.

Download your copy by visiting:

www.eatweeds.co.uk/photo-identification-guide

INTRODUCTION

For over fifteen years I have experimented and explored the world of wild plants. Uncovering how our ancestors used plants to nourish and heal themselves.

I've spent thousands of hours digging through scientific papers, read hundreds of books. Even gone so far as to be nomadic for over a year. During this time I followed the seasons and plants around the highways and byways of these isles.

I have written this book to help you rediscover our forgotten plant heritage. To learn how to use wild plants as food and medicine. Knowledge that was once common to everyone.

ALEXANDERS

SMYRNIUM OLUSATRUM

A native of Mediterranean Europe and naturalised in Britain since the days of the Romans, alexanders was the parsley of Alexandria, or *petroselinum Alexandrinum*, in medieval Latin.

This forgotten plant, once popular in ancient kitchen gardens, now thrives in abundance by the sea. It was cultivated for centuries as a common table vegetable across Europe until it was eventually replaced by the milder-tasting celery.

Like many members of the Apiaceae family, alexanders exudes aromatic oils with a pungent, sweet smell that attracts a wide range of pollinating insects.

There is some evidence that the Romans brought it to Britain to use as a culinary and medicinal herb because of its aromatic parts. According to Pliny (70 AD), it gained the name *Smyrnium* because of the distinctive myrrh-like fragrance of the fruits; the thickened tap root is also fragrant.

Alexanders appears to have been dismissed in folklore much

earlier than it was dismissed at the kitchen table – stories or customs relating to the plant are few and far between.

PARTS USED FOR FOOD

Leaves, stem, flowers, root.

FOOD USES

Alexanders was once known as 'black potherb' because of its black, spicy seeds.

It is often found growing in ancient monastic ruins, having been cultivated as a kitchen garden herb by monks.

The leaves and stalks can be blanched or steamed to add to soups, broths and stews.

The flowers can be added as a spice and decoration to salads. The buds can be eaten pickled or fried.

The root can be used in a similar way to parsnip in casseroles and stews.

NUTRITIONAL PROFILE

The fruits are a rich source of protein, carbohydrates and fatty acids. The plant contains flavonoids and other bioactive compounds (Bertoli et al., 2004).

HERBAL MEDICINE USES

Alexanders was traditionally used for cleansing the blood and as a digestive herb for strengthening the stomach.

Seafarers used it to treat scurvy, while herbalists used it to relieve stomach and urinary problems.

It was also a remedy for headaches, toothaches, swellings of the body, cuts and bruises, asthma and consumption (tuberculosis).

CAUTIONS

There is little data about the plant's toxicity.

BLACK MUSTARD

BRASSICA NIGRA

This intrepid plant has trekked its way across the world and is now cultivated across Europe and in the Middle East, Russia, China, India and South Africa.

It is thought to have been introduced to Britain in 1720, but it may have been known as a condiment in eastern parts of the Roman Empire, according to an Edict on Maximum Prices issued by Roman Emperor Diocletian in 301 AD.

The name 'mustard' is thought to derive from the Latin *mustem*, meaning 'must' (fermenting grape juice), and *ardens*, meaning 'burning' and referring to the hotness of the plant.

PARTS USED FOR FOOD

Leaves, flowers, seed.

FOOD USES

Black mustard was known to the Egyptians and Greeks as a plant which could be used in a similar way to spinach, and which also has flavoursome seeds.

The Romans are credited with making black mustard into a sauce, and also for using the coarse herb as a pickling spice and table condiment.

In medieval England, mustard was used to flavour a sauce of honey and olive oil that was drizzled over meat dishes.

Pungent and spicy, the peppery seeds are a common seasoning for pickles, sausages and sauerkraut.

The seeds can be ground into 'mustard powder' which is a popular ingredient of curry powders in Eastern cooking.

Black mustard seeds add more than flavour to food. They stimulate the appetite before or during a meal and as a digestive (aiding digestion after a meal).

The young shoots or leaves can be tossed in salads and eaten raw, or cooked as a potherb.

The budding flowering tops can be cooked and used in recipes in a similar way to broccoli.

In Mediterranean countries, black mustard is commonly gathered with other cruciferous vegetables and traditionally boiled, then eaten with olive oil, lemon juice and salt.

NUTRITIONAL PROFILE

Nutritionally, black mustard has potent antioxidant activity, which can help to reduce the incidence of many chronic diseases when included as part of a balanced diet.

Studies have shown that *B. nigra* contains 97 mg of vitamin C per 100 g, while it doesn't skimp on other nutrients either; the fresh weight of 100 g plant material contains 183 mg calcium, 50 mg phosphorus, 3 mg iron (Kuhnlein, 1991).

HERBAL MEDICINE USES

Hippocrates, a Greek physician who was hailed as the father of medicine, wrote about the medicinal actions of black mustard in 450 BC.

The plant was used by the ancient Greeks and by the Chinese for thousands of years in food and medicine.

Early herbal texts recommend mustard for treating a wide range of conditions from alopecia and epilepsy to toothache and snakebites.

The seeds were thought to be good for lethargy and stomach complaints, and as a blood purifier.

Mustard poultices, or 'plasters', have long been used to treat rheumatism and sciatica.

While black mustard is not native to North America, the American Indians used it as a medicinal plant, for instance grinding the seeds into a snuff for head colds.

The Mohegans used the herb to treat headaches and toothache. It was also adopted by early settlers to make an ointment for rheumatic pain.

Mexican Indians used mustard oil as a children's cough remedy, rubbing it on the chest and covering with a flannel cloth.

CAUTIONS

Black mustard is a powerful-acting plant and may cause irritation internally to the gut or externally to skin. Use with caution and in moderation.

3

BRAMBLE OR BLACKBERRY

RUBUS FRUTICOSUS AGG.

This thorny bush often gets overlooked and is underappreciated until it starts to produce its fruit. Traditionally, blackberry picking was a popular late summer activity for many people in Britain, Ireland and other European countries.

In the West Country of England, blackberries are called 'moochers', referring to 'mooching' or 'playing truant', as they distracted children from getting to school. The thorny bramble has always been the friend of poor people, because of the wool it 'collects' from sheep. Country women made the wool into mops to sell for a few pence.

The name of the bramble bush apparently derives from 'brambel' or 'brymbyl', meaning prickly, while 'fruticosus' comes from the Latin for 'shrubby'.

Tales have been told about the blackberry since the earliest times:

Jonathan ... upbraided the men of Shechem for their ingratitude to his father's house, relating to them the parable of the trees choosing a king, the humble bramble being finally elected, after the olive, fig-tree and vine had refused the dignity (Grieve, 1931).

PARTS USED FOR FOOD

Leaves, shoots, fruit, root.

FOOD USES

Blackberry picking is a popular pastime in late summer and early autumn in Britain and Ireland. Many people in towns and villages will walk along waysides and hedgerows to fill their buckets with blackberries to eat, cook and freeze. However, this is not a modern pastime.

Blackberries have been eaten since early human history. The seeds were found in the stomach of a Neolithic man dug up in Walton-on-the-Naze, Essex. They have been used as a food source almost worldwide.

Today the fruit is one of the most widely collected wild edibles. Blackberries are used to make jams, jellies, wine, liqueurs and pie fillings. They can be mixed with crab apples to make fruit cheeses, made into savoury-sweet condiments, such as pickles, chutneys and ketchup, and used to flavour vinegar. In seventeenth-century England, blackberry was drunk as a cordial with spices and brandy.

The leaves are used for tea. The young shoots, either cooked or raw, can be added to omelettes or eaten with olive oil and lemon juice, or even with fish eggs.

Blackberry blossom is a useful source of nectar for bees too. Honeybees forage on the flowers to produce a light-flavoured, fruity honey.

NUTRITIONAL PROFILE

Some varieties of blackberries have more dietary fibre than whole-meal bread (Mabey, 1972).

Blackberries are also a very good source of vitamin C, containing around 15 mg per 100 g. They are about 5% sugar (Vaughan and Geissler, 2009).

The first berries that ripen are said to be the sweetest and juiciest, whereas smaller berries further up the stalk that ripen later may be 'seedy'.

HERBAL MEDICINE USES

Herbalists have recommended blackberry jelly, cordial or wine for its potent restorative powers. Nicholas Culpeper, 17th-century English botanist, physician and astrologer, praised the plant as a remedy for almost all ailments, from wounds and ulcers to fevers and itching.

In Irish folk medicine, bramble leaves, roots and fruits were a common remedy for ailments such as colds, coughs and flu, because of their astringent and antiseptic properties.

Bramble has also been used to treat sore feet, cuts, burns, ulcers, kidney problems and diarrhoea. There were various remedies; bramble juice was mixed with butter to treat swellings, and black-berry vinegar was taken to treat fevers, colds, gout and arthritis.

CAUTIONS

There are few concerns about using bramble in food and medicine.

4

BROOKLIME

VERONICA BECCABUNGA

Brooklime is a delicate blue flower of ponds and streams, and often grows with watercress. It was used for centuries as a salad plant in northern Europe, collected in spring. It is well known for its pungency and bitterness.

Indeed, its species name, beccabunga, means 'pungent', possibly coming from the Flemish beckpunge, meaning 'mouth smart'. The 'lime' in its common name is thought to be derived from an Anglo-Saxon word for the mud in which it grows.

PARTS USED FOR FOOD

Leaves.

FOOD USES

Bitter-tasting brooklime can be eaten like watercress, added raw to salads, or 'boiled and steamed like a potherb'.

This wild edible is best mixed with strongly-flavoured greens to compensate and complement its bitterness.

It can be brewed as a tea, called *tea de l'europe* (or European tea), which has a flavour similar to Chinese green tea.

NUTRITIONAL PROFILE

Brooklime is rich in vitamin C and antioxidants such as flavonoids and phenolics, which help to reduce incidences of chronic disease when eaten as part of our diet (Guarrera and Savo, 2016).

Kuhnlein (1991) suggests that European brooklime also contains 3.8 g of protein per 100 g of fresh weight.

HERBAL MEDICINE USES

Traditionally, brooklime was used as a diuretic treatment for jaundice, urinary and kidney ailments, as an expectorant for coughs and colds, and as a cure for scurvy.

Today we know that the plant contains vitamin C, as well as a glucoside (aucubin) and various other substances, such as sulphur.

CAUTIONS

There have been concerns about eating brooklime raw or lightly cooked, because it grows in nitrogen-rich habitats where liver fluke – a parasite that affects the liver – is present.

5

BURDOCK

ARCTIUM SPP.

Burdock is as heavily steeped in folk lore as some other wild plants. There is however an old custom in South Queensferry, Scotland whose origins have been lost in the mists of time. On the second Friday of August a man covered from head to ankles in the burrs of Burdock walks a seven-mile route, visiting every public house and drinking copious amounts of whisky. It is believed the ceremony was intended to ward off evil spirits, and that the Burryman is a symbol of rebirth, regeneration and fertility.

Although not always so punishing an encounter with burdock's prickly burs is often a memorable experience. It has always been popular with children, who delight in throwing the sticky burs at each other. These childhood games have no doubt helped to spread burdock far and wide.

Nicholas Culpeper wrote:

> It is so well known even to the little Boys, who pull off the Burs to throw and stick upon one another, that I spare to write any description of it (Grigson, 1955).

It was rumoured among country lads that they could catch bats with burdock.

There are many members of the genus *Arctium*, which is part of the Asteraceae family. The two species described here are the greater (*Arctium lappa*) and lesser burdock (*Arctium minus*).

There is a misconception in literature that greater burdock is the larger of the two plants, but the two species are relatively the same size and height. It is the burs of *A. lappa* that are big.

Its widely variable appearance, including a difference in the size of the flower heads on which a white cotton-like substance may be abundant or absent, has given rise to descriptions of different subspecies or species by botanists.

Burdock's Latin name *Arctium* is said to derive from the Greek *arktos*, meaning 'bear', and *lappa*, meaning 'to seize'. Another source suggests *lappa* comes from the Celtic *llap*, meaning 'a hand', because the plant seemingly appears to 'grip' passers-by. An old English name '*Herrif*', '*Aireve*', or '*Airup*' is rooted in the Anglo-Saxon *reafian*, also meaning 'to seize'.

The common name of the seedhead we are familiar with today, the English 'bur' or 'burr', may have originated from the French *bourre*, meaning 'woolly'. The word 'bur' also sounds like beurre or 'butter', echoing the old farm custom of wrapping butter in the large leaves to keep it cool. The plant's resemblance to dock, literally seen as a 'dock with burs', led to its name: bur-dock.

PARTS USED FOR FOOD

Leaf stalk, flower stem, root.

FOOD USES

Burdock roots can be eaten cooked as a boiled or fried vegetable and are truly delicious. They are more commonly used in Asian countries such as Japan and China.

The leaf stalk harvested during the second-year growth, just as the flower stem is budding, is passable but nothing to write home about.

The actual leaf, although mentioned in many books as edible, to my taste is utterly revolting.

One of the most delicious parts to eat is the pith found in the middle of the flower stalk. It is best to wait to scrape until you are in your kitchen, when the flesh can be put in lemon or vinegar water to prevent oxidisation.

NUTRITIONAL PROFILE

Contains vitamin C as one of its most valuable nutrients.

TRADITIONAL MEDICINE USES

Primarily thought of as a blood purifier and used as a herbal remedy for skin diseases and infections.

CAUTIONS

May cause contact dermatitis. The plant is best avoided in pregnancy due to oestrogen effects. Burdock may also interfere with some medications (Duke, 2002).

6

CHARLOCK

SINAPIS ARVENSIS

The seeds of charlock can live for at least eleven years and perhaps as many as fifty, buried in the ground, according to GE Fogg in the *Journal of Ecology*, Vol. 38, No 2, 1950.

In times past, charlock's prolific nature was its main virtue as a wild edible. The plant could not escape notice and there was plenty of it to harvest when other crops were scarce. In this way, *S. avensis* may have forced itself onto our plates. Caleb Threlkeld wrote in 1727:

> *It is called about the Streets of Dublin before the Flowers blow, by the name of Corn-cail, and used for boiled sallet'*

In the 17th century, Irish herbalist K'eogh also wrote:

> *[charlock] was boiled and eaten by the common people in spring.*

PARTS USED FOR FOOD

Leaves, flowers and seed.

FOOD USES

Charlock has a reputation as a famine food. In Ireland, it was used to make meal, porridge or gruel.

The sprouted seeds have a hot flavour and can be added to salads and sandwiches. The chopped leaves can be used as a herb, the flowers as a garnish and the larger leaves as a potherb.

The flower buds taste like radish and can be cooked and served like broccoli.

NUTRITIONAL PROFILE

The seeds contain fatty acids and the plant may also have antioxidant activity.

HERBAL MEDICINE USES

In Irish folk medicine, charlock was used as a cure for jaundice, to treat convulsions and cramps, and to cure coughs.

In County Limerick, charlock was juiced as a spring tonic and drunk to keep the body 'disease-free' for the rest of the year.

OTHER USES

The seed oil has been used to make soap and as a burning oil for lamps.

CAUTIONS

There is little information about toxicity and side effects.

7

CHICKWEED

STELLARIA MEDIA

Little birds in cages (especially Linnets) are refreshed with the lesser Chickeweed when they loath their meat. - John Gerard

Chickweed, like many wild plants, is a record of our past. Its seeds have been found in Neolithic burial sites and it is documented as an ancient potherb.

John Gerard (1545–1612), English herbalist, described thirteen species of chickweed, which are considered today to be variations of one type.

Chickweed earned its common name from the custom of using the seeds to feed birds. Germanic people called the weed *Huhnerdarm*, meaning 'hen's guts', and *Vogelkraut*, meaning 'bird plant'. In France, its names included *mouron, mouron dex oiseaux*, and *morsgeline*, from *Morsus gallinae*, or 'hen's bite'.

The Latin name *Stellaria* is more romantic, and originated from Swedish botanist Linnaeus' comparison of the plant's delicate, white flowers to tiny stars.

PARTS USED FOR FOOD

Leaves, stem.

FOOD USES

Chickweed can be boiled and eaten as a green vegetable much like spinach. In the past, the plant was used as a potherb by farming communities in Europe and Asia.

The leaves can also be eaten raw as a savoury herb in salads and sandwiches, or chopped and added to soups, omelettes, stuffing, meatballs or pies, or used as a garnish.

NUTRITIONAL PROFILE

Chickweed is a good source of vitamin C. It also contains vitamin A as well as B vitamins, fatty acids and minerals.

HERBAL MEDICINE USES

The plant has been widely used as an anti-inflammatory herb. For example, chickweed cream has been used to soothe eczema, sunburn and insect stings as well as to draw out boils and splinters.

OTHER USES

Yields lilac dyes for woollens.

CAUTIONS

May cause allergic reactions in some people (Mills and Bone, 2005).

8

CHICORY

CICHORIUM INTYBUS

Considered by some to be a weed and by others to be a beautiful wildflower, chicory was once cultivated as a vegetable.

As far back as Ancient Egypt and Rome, the roots were gathered as a table vegetable. Chicory is mentioned in the texts of Horace, Virgil, Ovid and Pliny.

It is described in the Papyrus Ebers, an Egyptian medical papyrus of herbal knowledge, thought to date from over 3,500 years ago. This may be the first written mention of the plant.

Chicory has been cultivated in European gardens since the 17th century for the leaves that are eaten in salads or cooked as a vegetable, and for the roots that are also used as a vegetable or chopped and roasted as a coffee substitute.

Ernst Small (Small, 2006) writes:

> *...chicory was not domesticated until 1845 at the Botanical Gardens in Brussels. That form became known as "witloof," Flemish for "white leaf." Cultivation was so successful that by 1875, roots were exported to France*

for consumption. By 1899, chicory leaf production was a new enterprise in the United States.

Among the famous persons who valued the plant were Charlemagne, who demanded that chicory be one of the seventy-five herbs planted in his gardens, and Elizabeth I, who drank a broth made from it.

PARTS USED FOR FOOD

Leaves, flowers, heart, root.

FOOD USES

Bitter-tasting chicory leaves add a sharp taste to salads or an extra bite to soups and stews.

Both chicory hearts and roots can be cooked as a vegetable and served with butter or cheese sauce.

The blue flowers can be added to salads, fresh or pickled, or crystallised and used as an edible decoration.

This wild edible is most famous for its roots which have been used for centuries to make chicory coffee, or as an adulterant of coffee.

NUTRITIONAL PROFILE

Chicory contains proteins; vitamins A, B, C and K; minerals including calcium, potassium and iron; and latex.

HERBAL MEDICINE USES

Since ancient times, chicory has been used as a herb to purify the blood and to cure liver and heart problems. The roots contain a bitter substance intybin which is sedative and has analgesic properties.

OTHER USES

In Arabia, chicory leaves were once burnt and used as insect repellent.

CAUTIONS

Drinking chicory regularly may impair digestion, and long-term use of chicory-root coffee can cause visual weakness in the retina. This is not a herb to take in excess (Karalliedde et al., 2008).

9

CLEAVERS OR GOOSEGRASS

GALIUM APARINE

Cleavers got its name from its tendency to cling to clothing and fur, enabling it to hitch a lift from any unsuspecting human or animal. It is no doubt as familiar as burdock to pet owners who have spent hours detangling cats and dogs from both bristly plants.

As a common weed, it was known by many local names:

> Its frequent name, Goosegrass, is a reference to the fact that geese are extremely fond of the herb. It is often collected for the purpose of giving it to poultry. Horses, cows and sheep will also eat it with relish (Grieve, 1931).

The weed was sometimes called 'loveman', which might be a loose translation of the Greek *philanthropon* or 'loving humankind'.

Swedish botanist Carl Linnaeus (1707-78) called the plant *aparine*, originating from the Greek *aparo*, 'to seize', likely referring to its clinging qualities.

Its botanical title *Galium* is thought to derive from the Greek 'milk', referring to its ability to curdle milk, and is the origin of another common name: 'bedstraw'.

PARTS USED FOR FOOD

Stems, leaves, seeds.

FOOD USES

Cleavers was once used as a potherb. It was a useful plant in medieval kitchens because it could be picked in frost or snow.

The plant's hook-like bristles soften when boiled. Its chopped leaves and stem can be made into soups and stews. The tender shoots can be boiled and buttered as a vegetable.

Cleavers belongs to the coffee family and its seeds have been ground to make cleavers coffee.

Sources suggest that caffeine quantities in cleavers are at least an order of magnitude lower than in coffee:

> *Coffee has caffeic acid from 1200 to 2500 mg per 100 g* (Kreicbergs et al., 2011).

> *...the total Caffeic acid derivatives was 0.348 ± 0.09 g, caffeic acid equivalents /100 g dry mass* (Al-Snafi, 2018).

So if you were thinking of making a 'cleavers espresso', you're out of luck!

NUTRITIONAL PROFILE

The whole plant is rich in vitamin C.

HERBAL MEDICINE USES

Cleavers has long been used as a slimming aid, probably because of its diuretic properties.

Worldwide, cleavers' most common use has been as a 'cleansing' herb for treating ailments, from kidney and urinary disorders to infections and itching.

OTHER USES

The sticky seeds were used by lacemakers to enlarge pinheads, and the root yielded a red dye.

Here's an unusual nugget of interest: the plant can turn birds' bones red if they eat its root.

CAUTIONS

There is little data about its safety profile. However it may cause severe skin irritation in some people (Karalliedde et al., 2008).

COW PARSLEY

ANTHRISCUS SYLVESTRIS

A common roadside plant in Britain, cow parsley has delicate, parsley-like leaves and white, umbrella-like clusters of flowers.

As one of the first *Umbellifer* flowers to appear in spring, Richard Mabey in *Plants With A Purpose* writes of it with affection:

> *No plant shapes our roadside landscape more than cow parsley. In May its lacy white flowers teem along every path and hedgebank.*

It is a plant that appears to have been overlooked in folk history, which could be due to its close resemblance to other species in the Umbellifer family, such as the poisonous hemlock (*Conium maculatum*) and fool's parsley (*Aethusa cynapium*).

Perhaps people avoided cow parsley fearing it as a deadly plant – it is not. Still, it is important to differentiate cow parsley from its notorious relatives.

I have created a fifteen-minute video that walks you through the differences between cow parsley and hemlock, which you can find at *eatweeds.co.uk/is-it-hemlock-or-cow-parsley*.

The genus name *Anthriscus* is thought to originate from the Greek for chervil, which has been used as a spice since ancient times. *Anthriscus sylvestris* means 'chervil from the woods'.

PARTS USED FOR FOOD

Leaves, stem, root.

FOOD USES

Cow parsley is closely related to chervil (*Anthriscus cerefolium*), and has a mildly spicy flavour.

The leaves can be used fresh or dried, sprinkled as seasoning in soups, omelettes, casseroles, potato and bean dishes. They can also be preserved in salt for future use. They make an excellent garnish in place of chervil for salads, potatoes and egg dishes

The young leaves can be cooked as a potherb and the roots are also edible.

NUTRITIONAL PROFILE

Research suggests that cow parsley demonstrates strong antioxidant activity and could have potential as a future health food or supplement.

HERBAL MEDICINE USES

Thanks to its poisonous lookalikes, cow parsley has seldom been used as a medicinal plant. When it was used as a remedy, this was often for kidney or urinary stones.

OTHER USES

The yellow-green dye used in the making of Harris tweed was traditional derived from the flowering tips of cow parsley.

CAUTIONS

The roots contain toxic compounds that could be dangerous if taken during pregnancy or when breastfeeding (Couplan, 1998).

However, I will state again as it is of the utmost importance: the greatest danger in using cow parsley as a wild edible is its close resemblance to deadly hemlock.

Do not pick hemlock by mistake – the consequences could be dire! Make sure you know how to identify your wild edibles.

IF IN DOUBT - LEAVE IT OUT

11

DAISY

BELLIS PERENNIS

The daisy stares at the sun all day long, but when it rains, or at night, the flower closes and droops its head.

This peculiarity has led to its most popular common name. Daisy is thought to be a corruption of the Anglo-Saxon *daeges*, meaning 'day', and *eage*, meaning 'eye', thus 'day's eye'. This became '*daysie*' or '*daysy*', and eventually '*dayses*' and 'daisies', as it was known by the time of great herbalists like Gerard and Culpeper.

This humble little flower is widespread in many parts of the world. It is a familiar childhood friend for those who remember sitting on the lawn 'sewing' daisy together, pulling each new stem through a split in the last.

This humble little flower is widespread in many parts of the world. It is a familiar childhood friend for those who remember sitting on the lawn 'sewing' daisy together, by pulling each new stem through a split in the last.

In Ireland, these charming daisy chains were called fairy chains. Sometimes a chain was also made by threading the flower heads onto a rush. In Scotland, the flower was called *bairnwort* because children were so fond of it.

Geoffrey Chaucer was said to be especially fond of daisies - so much so that he left his sick bed to visit the flowers, saying: 'That blissful sighte softeneth all my sorwe.' In his work *The Legend of Good Women*, he wrote:

> *Of all the flowers in the meadow, I most love those white and red flowers which men in our town call day's-eyes. For them I have such affection, as I have said, that when May is come, no day dawns upon me in my bed, but I am up and walking in the mead to see these flowers opening to the sun when it rises, in the bright morn, and through the long day thus I walk in the green.*

In the language of flowers, a wild daisy means: 'Expect my answer within a few days', while the old idiom 'pushing up daisies' means to be dead and buried.

It is a charming little plant that even superstition cannot tarnish. We look forward to seeing daisies in spring and, as Culpeper would say, we are so familiar with the flower that it needs no description.

PARTS USED FOR FOOD

Flower, leaves.

FOOD USES

The young flower heads or buds of daisies can be added to salads, soups or sandwiches; or the flower heads used to decorate salad dishes.

The leaves can be eaten raw despite their bitter aftertaste, preferably mixed in salad. They can also be cooked, and might be used as a potherb.

The buds can be preserved in vinegar and used in cooking as a substitute for capers.

NUTRITIONAL PROFILE

Daisy is both an anti-inflammatory herb and a vulnerary herb (used to improve circulation). Drink daisy tea for its health-giving and restorative properties.

A study of the nutritional value of wild plants during the war in Bosnia and Herzegovina (1992–95) found that daisies contained 34 mg of vitamin C per 100 g (Redzić, 2010).

HERBAL MEDICINE USES

The daisy was recognised as a medicinal herb from the 15th century onwards. The Flemish herbalist Robert Dodoens, or Dodonaeus, (1517–1585) wrote:

> *Daisies boiled in water, either the whole plant or just the flowers, and especially the small or wild (species), are good for fever, heating up the liver and all internal organs. This same herb in food or soups stimulates the movement of the bowels.*

By the 17th century, the daisy also had a reputation for healing broken bones, which is perhaps where it got the name 'bone flower'. The English naturalist William Turner (1509/10–1568) knew the daisy as 'banwort', 'because it helpeth bones to knyt againe'.

In Irish folk medicine, the daisy was used for all manner of conditions, as Gerard would have approved, including scrofula, tuberculosis, pleurisy, coughs, colds, headaches, stomach and liver complaints, and various skin problems from chilblains to ringworm. It was also made into a lotion for weak eyes and an ointment for burns, as in other parts of Britain.

OTHER USES

While the daisy has been less admired for its taste, its pretty flowers are always a crowd pleaser.

Daisies can be frosted and sprinkled on cakes for decoration or added to a cup of boiled water for a beautiful tea – sweetened with honey.

CAUTIONS

Few side effects are recorded from the use of daisies in food or medicine. However, it may cause an allergic reaction in people who are sensitive to the Asteraceae/Compositae plant family.

1 2

DANDELION

TARAXICUM OFFICINALE

The dandelion is a very common garden weed, scattering lawns everywhere with bright yellow flowers in spring. Once a cure-all of herbal medicine, it later came to be regarded as a nuisance to be vigorously dug up by gardeners.

Today the dandelion is enjoying a comeback as a cosmopolitan weed used in various herbal remedies and culinary dishes worldwide.

PARTS USED FOR FOOD

Roots, leaves, stem, buds and flowers.

FOOD USES

Dandelion-and-burdock is a popular fizzy drink made from the roots of the plant in the north of England. Dandelion root has also traditionally been used to make a coffee substitute.

The leaves are considered to be very nutritious and can be eaten as a salad or fresh vegetable. In Asian cooking, for example, dandelion leaves are used like lettuce, boiled, made into soup or fried.

The flower buds can be added to omelettes and fritters, the flowers baked into cakes, and even the pollen sprinkled on food for decoration and colouring.

Dandelion blossoms make a delicious country wine, and a beer can be brewed from the whole plant before it flowers.

NUTRITIONAL PROFILE

Dandelion 'greens' contain vitamins A, C, E, K, B6, beta carotene, folate, thiamine, riboflavin, calcium, iron, potassium and manganese.

HERBAL MEDICINE USES

Dandelion has been used as a herbal medicine to treat wide-ranging conditions, including stomach and liver complaints, diabetes, heart problems, anaemia, respiratory ailments, consumption (tuberculosis), toothache, broken bones and sprains, sore eyes, cuts and nervousness.

OTHER USES

Dandelion provides a rich source of nectar and pollen for bees and other pollinating insects, from early spring to late autumn.

CAUTIONS

As a member of the same plant family as ragwort and daisy, dandelion may potentially cause allergies. However, there are few documented cases of the plant's toxicity in humans.

13

DOCK

RUMEX SPP.

Docks in various shapes and sizes have grown in Britain since three ice ages ago, and remains of dock have been found in places where people such as the ancient Celts once farmed.

Curly dock (*Rumex crispus*) and broad-leaved dock (*Rumex obtusifolius*), have both been used in food and medicine for many centuries.

PARTS USED FOR FOOD

Leaves, stems, flowers.

FOOD USES

Docks have lemony-tasting leaves which add a tang to cooked dishes. It is often agreed that the youngest plants are best and make a tasty 'spinach', while others find the taste of docks 'sour' but 'hearty'.

Serve dock greens with butter, bacon, hard-boiled eggs and

seasoning. The leaves can also be stuffed like vine leaves with a rice, herb and cheese filling.

Dried dock can be used as seasoning for rice, potatoes, seafood or sandwich spread.

Docks produce large quantities of fruits and seeds, which can be boiled into a mush or ground and added to flour or meal for making breads, muffins and gravies.

The stems of young dock plants can be chopped, simmered and sweetened with honey as a substitute for rhubarb, for instance as a pie filling.

NUTRITIONAL PROFILE

Docks are very nutritious. Curly dock, for example, contains more vitamin C than oranges and more vitamin A than carrots. It also contains vitamins B1 and B2, and iron.

HERBAL MEDICINE USES

Dock leaves are famously used to soothe nettle stings and often grow near the offending plant. However one must spit on the leaf first before applying it, as 'the enzymes in saliva actually release some of the anti-inflammatory properties of the leaf' (Hatfield, 2008).

The cooling properties of docks have also been used to soothe insect bites and stings, as well as scalds, blisters and sprains.

Docks leaves were wrapped around minor wounds to staunch bleeding, and an infusion of the roots drunk for purifying the blood.

The juice from the leaves can be applied as a compress to heal bruises.

The seeds have been used to treat coughs, colds and bronchitis, and the roots used as a remedy for jaundice, liver problems, skin ailments, boils, rheumatism, constipation and diarrhoea.

OTHER USES

Dock seed heads are an important source of food for wildlife in winter, such as birds, rodents and deer. They are also decorative and can be collected for ornamental flower arrangements.

CAUTIONS

Docks contain oxalic acid, which can be toxic if taken in excessive amounts. Some texts suggest that eating docks or ingesting them as medicine should be avoided during pregnancy and when breast-feeding.

Docks can trigger hayfever or aggravate asthma in some people.

14

FAT HEN

CHENOPODIUM ALBUM

Fat hen has been used as a wild vegetable since ancient times in Europe, and its remains have been found in Bronze Age sites in Britain, and in pre-Norman sites in Ireland.

According to several sources, it was among the commonest wild 'spinach' plants. However, the introduction of spinach from south-west Asia eventually replaced fat hen in British and European cooking; while in America, the introduction of maize and beans gradually replaced its use.

PARTS USED FOR FOOD

Leaves, seeds.

FOOD USES

The seeds are rich in starch. They can be ground and added to flour to bake breads, cakes, biscuits, pancakes or muffins. Alternatively, add the seeds to salads or stir fries, either sprouted or as they are.

The leaves and young stem tips can be used as a spinach substitute. The tender leaves can also be used to make salads, stir fries, sauces or pesto.

The water in which the tender greens are cooked can be saved and drunk as a nutritional broth, or frozen in stock cubes.

The young flower buds can be cooked and eaten by steaming and tossing in butter like broccoli.

NUTRITIONAL PROFILE

Fat hen is rich in protein, vitamins A, B1, B2, B3 (niacin) and C, as well as calcium, phosphorus, iron, and omega-3 fatty acids (Mabey, 1972). The seeds of some *Chenopodium* species are higher in lipids, and nutrients such as calcium and magnesium, than many other seeds and grains (Pachauri et al., 2012).

HERBAL MEDICINE USES

Fat Hen is occasionally mentioned in old herbals as a treatment for ailments of the times, such as scurvy, sores and gout. The plant is sometimes still used to treat inflammation, rheumatism or toothache.

CAUTIONS

Some herbalists suggest that the seeds of *Chenopodium spp.* may be toxic if eaten in excess, while others go as far as to say that the seeds should not be eaten at all because of their high saponin content, and that they may pose a risk to people suffering from arthritis, rheumatism, liver disease or intestinal inflammations.

The greens too may contain oxalic acid which could affect calcium absorption, or cause mouth irritation when eaten raw or in excess.

Take care also not to mistakenly identify lookalike plant black nightshade (*Solanum nigrum*), which is poisonous.

15

GARLIC MUSTARD

ALLIARIA PETIOLATA

Learning the history and folklore of a plant somehow makes it more attractive for culinary use, but garlic mustard has attracted little folklore except that inferred by its various common names: beggarman's oatmeal, Jack-by-the-hedge, mustard root, sauce alone, stinking hedge mustard, to name a few.

Though unrelated to garlic, *A. petiolata* gives off a garlic-like smell when its leaves are bruised or chopped.

A common wild herb in Britain and Ireland, it is found across Europe, where it appears largely forgotten, and it was introduced to North America, where it is largely seen as an invasive weed.

With its heart-shaped rosette of leaves and bright-white, cross-shaped flowers, one would imagine it to be a plant steeped in fairy romance and early Christian legend. Instead, this wild herb appears to be missing its place in folklore.

PARTS USED FOR FOOD

Leaves, stem, seeds, root.

FOOD USES

The release of a garlic smell and taste when the leaves are crushed led to the use of garlic mustard as an alternative to true garlic. It has the same uses as garlic in food preparation and cooking.

The wild herb also makes an excellent savoury salad green, sauce and potherb.

NUTRITIONAL PROFILE

As a member of the mustard family, which includes cabbage, cauliflower, broccoli, brussels sprouts, mustard and watercress, garlic mustard contains the cancer-preventing chemicals isothiocyanates. It is therefore among those vegetables which, if eaten as part of a healthy, balanced diet, might help to prevent cancer.

Garlic mustard also contains allyl sulfides from the garlic family.

HERBAL MEDICINE USES

Garlic mustard has been used as an antiseptic herb for treating leg ulcers, bruises and sores, coughs and colds. It has also been used to clear a stuffy head, to encourage sweating and even as a cure for colic and kidney stones.

In Somerset, England, the fresh green leaves were rubbed on feet to relieve cramp.

OTHER USES

A yellow dye might also be obtained from the whole plant.

CAUTIONS

Garlic mustard is apparently 'palatable to livestock' (Quattrocchi, 2012), which suggests another means to manage its spread on the borders of fields and woodlands. An unfortunate side effect of this, however, is that it can lend a disagreeable flavour to cows' milk, and an unpleasant taste to poultry meat.

16

GLASSWORT OR SAMPHIRE

SALICORNIA EUROPAEA

A delicacy of the salt marshes, glasswort was named for the glass that was once made from its ashes. It grows abundantly in parts of Britain, where it forms 'samphire lawns'.

Its salt marsh home is an important habitat for wildlife, which means the popular plant can be found growing in protected areas.

PARTS USED FOR FOOD

Whole plant.

FOOD USES

The young shoots of glasswort make a crispy salad green or can be lightly boiled and served with butter as a side dish.

The shoots can even be picked and chewed straight from the marshes if you like the salty taste; otherwise it's preferable to wash the plant thoroughly in the kitchen.

The whole plant can be treated as a side vegetable or made into a pickle.

NUTRITIONAL PROFILE

Glasswort contains various minerals, including potassium, manganese, calcium, silicon, boron and iodine, and is a source of vitamin C. The seeds are rich in protein.

HERBAL MEDICINE USES

Glasswort grew abundantly along the north Norfolk coast, England, and was collected to make an ointment for dry, cracked skin.

Historical and current herbal texts suggest that glasswort is an effective diuretic (to increase urination) and that it has purifying properties.

OTHER USES

The plant provides fodder for cattle that like to graze on the salty, succulent stems and branches. It is useful for binding and stabilising soil on vulnerable coastlines, which is one of its uses in the Netherlands.

CAUTIONS

Few precautions for eating glasswort or using the plant as a medicinal or culinary herb are noted.

17

GROUND ELDER

AEGOPODIUM PODAGRARIA

Several authorities suggest ground elder was most likely introduced to this country by medieval monks, who cultivated it as a medicinal plant. Other sources say that it arrived with the Romans and made itself useful as a potherb and as a treatment for gout.

Whatever its origins, within a few centuries ground elder had outstayed its welcome and come to be regarded as a nuisance weed, reluctant to give up its place in the herb garden. Its creeping, stubborn root system earned the name 'jump about' and 'farmer's plague' in some parts of Britain, because it spread vigorously and rapidly.

The English botanist John Gerard observed (1597):

> *Herbe Gerard groweth of itself in gardens without setting or sowing and is so fruitful in its increase that when it hath once taken roote, it will hardly be gotten out againe, spoiling and getting every yeare more ground, to the annoying of better herbes.*

PARTS USED FOR FOOD

Leaves, stalk, flowers.

FOOD USES

In the Middle Ages, ground elder was a potherb. In the markets of medieval Cracow, Poland, it was sold as a wild vegetable.

> *The young leaves in the spring are eaten in Sweden and Switzerland as greens (Lightfoot, 1792).*

In Anglo-Saxon Britain, ground elder was used to clarify beers, and may have been called 'gill' from the French *guiller*, meaning 'to ferment beer'.

In parts of the Ukraine, it is still used as an ingredient of green *borscht*, a soup made of green vegetables.

NUTRITIONAL PROFILE

The young leaves contain high amounts of vitamin C and are best picked in spring for use in salads and soups.

HERBAL MEDICINE USES

Ground elder was once used as a medicinal plant for various ailments, but its primary purpose was as a cure for gout and to relieve pain and swelling. For this reason, the plant was also known as goutwort.

Modern herbals still recommend ground elder as a treatment for gout, sciatica, rheumatism, haemorrhoids, inflammation, and water retention.

OTHER USES

While we make little use of ground elder as a food plant today, it is sometimes used as a fodder for pigs and is therefore also known as pigweed.

CAUTIONS

There is little information on the side effects of ground elder.

18

GROUND IVY

GLECHOMA HEDERACEA

Ground ivy, a perennial plant with trailing dark-green, kidney-shaped leaves that retain their year-round colour, flourishes everywhere, from sunny banks to shady wastelands.

Its bluish flowers, with their purple tint, are seen in summer and autumn. 'Its popular name is attributed to the resemblance borne by its foliage to that of the true ivy' (Grieve, 1931).

The common name of ground ivy is misleading, because it is not a true ivy. However, the plant has a plethora of other names from which to choose: Gill-go-by-the-ground, Lizzy-run-up-the-hedge, cat's foot, Devil's candlesticks and alehoof, among others.

It was not considered particularly friendly to its countryside companions, being known to drive off other plants that grew near it. It was avoided by cattle and feared toxic to horses.

Yet it was a favourite ingredient in spells and magic, perhaps because it grew so readily in graveyards, ruins and shady places thought frequented by witches. The plant's strong association with witchcraft might partly explain why country-folk believed it drove away other flora.

Despite its dubious character, Chaucer, in the *Nun's Priest's Tale* (1392), describes it as 'Of herbe yve, growyng in oure yeerd, ther mery is.' I agree!

PARTS USED FOR FOOD

Shoots, leaves.

FOOD USES

In past times, ground ivy was used in brewing to flavour and clarify the beer.

A tea, called gill tea, was also made with ground ivy by steeping the plant in boiling water and sweetening with sugar, honey or liquorice.

The leaves and stem have an aromatic flavour and can be used to flavour soups and sauces, or egg or meat dishes, in place of mint or thyme.

The young shoots and leaves have also been eaten as bitter greens, like spinach, or added raw to salads.

NUTRITIONAL PROFILE

There is little data on ground ivy's nutritional content.

HERBAL MEDICINE USES

Ground ivy was largely used to relieve headaches, congestion, coughs and colds. An infused ale or beer was said to 'clear the head' due to its expectorant action.

An infusion of the herb, or the expressed juice, was also used to treat eye disease or injury.

OTHER USES

In the crossover between Pagan and Christian traditions, the plant was part of Green Thursday or Maundy Thursday celebrations. Crowns of green ivy were worn as people danced at night on Green Thursday to celebrate nature's return in spring and to reaffirm their connection to the old gods. Ground ivy was also an important ingredient in Maundy Thursday soup, served on the day that starts the holy period before Easter Sunday.

CAUTIONS

Ground ivy is suspected of poisoning grazing animals, such as cattle and horses, who are perhaps more at risk of excessive consumption.

There is limited data on the plant's toxicity in humans.

19

HIMALAYAN BALSAM

IMPATIENS GLANDULIFERA

When a beekeeper opens up the hive to see that many of the honeybee workers bear a strange white stripe, he knows that the colony has been foraging on Himalayan balsam.

The plant tempts the honeybee with its sweet nectar and provides a rich crop in summer. But as the insect crawls inside the flower, its sticky stamen leaves a white stripe on the bee's thorax.

Geoffrey Grigson (1955) generously describes the arrival of Himalayan balsam, often seen as an invasive species, in the UK:

> *Introduced in 1839, it was cultivated at first as a greenhouse annual by gardeners who never imagined the career ahead of it.*

Today, this native Indian plant may be a familiar sight along rivers and stream banks.

PARTS USED FOR FOOD

Only the seeds.

FOOD USES

The seeds can be eaten raw and taste like walnuts. They can also be cooked like lentils, and make a wonderful dahl.

NUTRITIONAL PROFILE

Himalayan balsam contains high levels of phenols and flavonoids, suggesting potential use as an antioxidant supplement for enhancing health.

HERBAL MEDICINE USES

The flowers are said to have cooling properties, and the leaves have been used to soothe burns.

The seeds are diuretic, and the root juice treats hematuria (blood in the urine).

OTHER USES

The seed oil can be used to make varnish.

CAUTIONS

There is little information about the plant's toxicity or side effects in food or medicine.

20

HOGWEED

HERACLEUM SPHONDYLIUM

Common hogweed - **not** giant hogweed *Heracleum mantegazzianum* - has enjoyed a reputation as both an important wild vegetable and a noxious weed.

The common name 'hogweed' refers to its popular use as fodder for livestock, particularly pigs, which might in part be due to its abundance in the countryside.

Phoebe Lankester, an English student of plant lore, is cited by Fernald and Kinsey (1996):

> *The leaves are collected and given to pigs, who quickly fatten upon them; hence the plant is called Hogweed.*

It is also a popular plant for insects, and its flowers are known to attract around 118 different insect visitors.

William Turner (1548):

> *'It may be called in Englishe Cow-persnepe or rough Persnepe'.*

PARTS USED FOR FOOD

Shoots, leaves, stalk, flower buds, seed, root.

FOOD USES

The whole plant can be boiled and eaten as a vegetable or potherb, in particular the leaves and shoots, which are said to taste like asparagus.

The leaves can be fried, or braised, in butter; they become crispy as the plant sugars caramelise.

Older leaves can be chopped up and used to make a stock, or to add flavour to dishes in the same way as bay leaves.

The young shoots can also be fried in butter or boiled for a light supper.

The flower buds can be cooked and served like broccoli with butter or white sauce.

The seeds have an orange-cardamom flavour used to spice puddings and syrups. They can be added to bean dishes when green.

The roots are strongly aromatic and can be prepared as a condiment, or added to other dishes as a flavouring.

NUTRITIONAL PROFILE

Hogweed contains 105 mg of vitamin C per 100 g of fresh leaves, while also containing 3.25 mg carotene. As an energy-sustaining vegetable, it contains (per 100 g) 5.31 g protein, 6.42 g carbohydrates and 50 calories (Pieroni, 2014).

TRADITIONAL MEDICINE USES

Hogweed was a folk remedy for many common complaints, such as jaundice, warts and sores.

The juice was applied to warts, and the pollen was dusted on sores.

The seeds and roots were also boiled and drunk to treat liver problems and jaundice.

In Irish folk medicine, hogweed was traditionally employed to stop bleeding.

OTHER USES

The hollow stems were once used as a cigarette substitute and smoked by gypsies.

CAUTIONS

Hogweed is known to cause photosensitive skin reactions, such as blistering, because of the plant's furanocoumarins.

It must be picked with gloves and never eaten raw or al dente.

I have had first-hand experiences of people having some pretty serious reactions to hogweed ... so tread cautiously!

Some texts list the plant as an emmenagogue, meaning it promotes menstrual bleeding, so it is best avoided during pregnancy.

HORSERADISH

ARMORACIA RUSTICANA

Horseradish has been cultivated since ancient times. It is thought to be indigenous to parts of Eastern Europe, with several authorities saying it originated in southern Russia and the Ukraine.

Other sources suggest it came to Britain as a spice plant from the Middle East in the 16th century, or that its true origins are lost in time.

Alphonse de Candolle (1959) promoted the theory that horseradish originated in temperate Eastern Europe, because it grew from 'Finland and Poland to the Caspian Sea and to the deserts of Cuman and in Turkey', but became more scattered towards Western Europe.

Its most primitive name, *chren,* was common in Slavic languages, which later became *kren, kreen,* and *cran* in old German and French dialects.

Horseradish entered the Materia Medica of the 18th-century London Pharmacopoeia as *Raphanus rusticanus.* (The Materia

Medica is a body of collected knowledge about the therapeutic properties of substances used in medicine.)

It belongs to the cruciferous (mustard) vegetable family, along with broccoli, cabbage and cauliflower, and has been used as a spice for over 2,000 years. It is sold for quite a high price when one considers it can be picked in the wild in abundance. But do remember that in Britain the law requires the landowner's permission before collecting any wild plant roots.

PARTS USED FOR FOOD

Leaves, roots, sprouted seeds.

FOOD USES

The fresh roots are used as a culinary herb in sauces, powders and vinegars, for flavouring meats and vegetables. They can also be preserved in vinegar or beet juice to make white or red pickles. The sauce is popular for accompanying roast beef, steaks and smoked fish; the flavour can be overpoweringly hot for some and it is best used sparingly. The roots can also be sliced and roasted as a vegetable.

The young leaves can be added to salads and pickles or cooked as a potherb.

The sprouted seeds can be used to season salads.

NUTRITIONAL PROFILE

As a cruciferous vegetable, horseradish may have beneficial antioxidant properties. However, much of its nutritional content is lost during cooking; its vitamin C denatures, and nutrients like vitamin K and calcium are cut by a half.

Cooking also removes the plant's pungency, as does a long period of refrigeration after preparation.

HERBAL MEDICINE USES

Horseradish is a warming herb, used to increase circulation and decrease swellings, and to promote urination. It is thought to be helpful for rheumatic conditions.

The strong, vaporous odour of the root, when broken, can be used to banish heavy colds.

OTHER USES

Some varieties are grown for their ornamental leaves. An infusion of horseradish leaves sprayed onto apple trees can prevent brown rot. Kept on the borders of vegetable patches, it assists in the growth of healthy and disease-resistant potatoes.

The foliage can be harvested to make a yellow dye.

The volatile oils in horseradish may be an effective insecticide.

CAUTIONS

Excessive doses of horseradish may cause gut irritation, diarrhoea and night sweats, or may irritate the skin (when applied externally).

The Commission E (a committee made up of scientists, toxicologists, doctors, and pharmacists) recommends that horseradish isn't taken by children under four years old, although there is no supporting evidence to back this up (Gardner et al., 2013).

The herb is listed as an abortifacient in some texts and may be best avoided in excess, or altogether during pregnancy (Quattrocchi, 2012).

22

LADY'S SMOCK OR CUCKOOFLOWER

CARDAMINE PRATENSIS

When the cuckoo calls in late spring and early summer, the cuckooflower's conspicuous blooms start to appear.

Lady's smock was also known as 'water cuckoo' or 'wet cuckoo', because of the plant's tendency to grow in damp places.

Its less flattering nickname of 'cuckoo's spit' (Watts, 2007), which referred to the froth covering a pale green insect found on the plant, meant that few children in the north of England would pick the wildflower, believing that the cuckoo had spat on it.

Its other popular name of 'lady's smock' may have arisen because the flowers were often seen on Lady Day (25 March).

Folklorist Margaret Baker wrote about the plant under the name of 'lady's smock', although she said it was known as 'cuckooflower' by milkmaids.

But this is only half the story. As Geoffrey Grigson (1955) writes, the cuckooflower is a 'spring flower associated with milkmaids and their smocks, the cuckoo, and the Virgin'.

While in many European countries, the plant was known as the cuckooflower, or some such other name that linked its flowering time to the cuckoo's song, in England its 'smock' and 'smick' nicknames were 'words of amorous looks and purposes' (Grigson, 1955). 'Smick-smock' was another common name for the flower.

From the Middle Ages, the word 'smock' referred to a woman's undergarments. By the 18th century, this became 'shift', and later, the more refined 'chemise'.

Thus, the cuckooflower was a plant in great need of Christianising and 'handing over to the Virgin' (Grigson, 1955).

Richard Folkard (1892) gives a slightly more tame explanation for the name 'Lady's smock', saying the plant was so-called because of the 'resemblance of its pale flowers to little smocks hung out to dry', adding, 'as they used to be once a year, at that season especially'.

PARTS USED FOR FOOD

Leaves, shoots, buds.

FOOD USES

Cuckooflower has a pungent flavour which some say is similar to watercress.

The leaves, shoots and flower buds can be added to salads, sandwiches and sauces, or served with oil and vinegar.

NUTRITIONAL PROFILE

Cuckooflower has a high content of vitamin C which supports the plant's traditional use as a treatment for scurvy.

HERBAL MEDICINE USES

In past times, as well as being used to treat scurvy, cuckooflower was employed as a remedy for fevers. It was also prescribed for kidney stones and ulcers, to aid digestion or stimulate the appetite, and as a diuretic.

OTHER USES

New research suggests that cuckooflowers possess diverse chemical compounds, including glucosinolates, flavonoids, phenolic acids, fatty acids, amino acids and other trace minerals. They have been shown to exhibit a wide range of actions including antibacterial, antidiabetic, antifungal, anti-infective, antiviral and antioxidant (Montaut and Bleeker, 2011). This suggests that the plant has many potential untapped uses.

CAUTIONS

There is little information about the side effects of taking cuckooflower as a food or medicine.

23

LESSER CELANDINE

RANUNCULUS FICARIA

The plant's glossy green foliage and shining yellow flowers inspired 19th-century poet William Wordsworth to praise its 'glittering countenance'.

One of the first heralds of spring, its beauty is brilliant and brief. The blossoms are at their best in March and April, but fade and wither by May.

Its botanical name, *Ranunculus ficaria,* refers to its place in the buttercup family *Ranunculus,* although botanists sometimes use the more distinct species name *Ficaria verna.*

Lesser celandine is unrelated to greater celandine (*Chelidonium majus*).

It appears we have Pliny to blame for the legend that gave rise to the name 'celandine', deriving from the Greek khelidon, meaning 'swallow'. The ancient Roman author claimed that birds used the plant to restore their sight, and centuries later, Greek philosopher Theophrastus wrote that the flower blooms when the 'swallow' wind blows.

PARTS USED FOR FOOD

Leaves, roots.

FOOD USES

The plant's roots swell up to form bulbs or tubers, which are delicious and can be eaten as a starchy vegetable.

Lesser celandine has been used as potherb in central Europe and the young parts of the plant have been added (cooked) to salads.

NUTRITIONAL PROFILE

Lesser celandine may contain antioxidants that make it worthy as a springtime tonic, although further research into its biological activities is needed.

HERBAL MEDICINE USES

Lesser celandine was a traditional remedy for piles; its common name of figwort alludes to 'fig' as an old name for the condition.

An ointment of the roots was also said to cure corns and warts.

OTHER USES

An unusual use for the petals and leaves, recorded in Cumbria, England, was for cleaning teeth.

CAUTIONS

As a member of the buttercup family, lesser celandine may cause contact dermatitis in humans and animals (Wyse Jackson, 2013).

The plant sap may also cause nausea and vomiting if taken raw internally (Karalliedde et al., 2008).

The plant is best avoided during pregnancy or when breastfeeding.

24

MALLOW

MALVA SYLVESTRIS

A Chinese poet in the first century BC wrote, 'I'll pluck the mallows and make soup.' (Waley and Bai, 1919)

The whole family of mallow is edible; the plants were eaten by the Egyptians and Syrians, the young shoots were cooked as a vegetable in ancient Rome, and in the Middle Ages, mallows were a common pot and salad herb.

The mallow family is widely used in food, medicine and other industries, as well as for ornamental garden plants, as it includes plants such as the hibiscus and hollyhock.

The mallow family name, Malvaceae, originates from the Greek malake (meaning 'soft') and refers to the 'special qualities of the Mallows in softening and healing' (Grieve, 1931).

Common mallow (*Malva sylvestris*) is named *sylvestris* (meaning 'wild from woods or forests').

The uses of mallow in food and medicine are largely interchange-able between the different species. It is likely that throughout history, one species has been preferred over another, or the rest, due to its ease of availability to the local community.

PARTS USED FOR FOOD

Leaves, flowers, roots and seeds.

FOOD USES

Common mallow yields disc-shaped seeds, or 'nutlets', that are edible and can be snacked on. They are traditionally referred to as 'cheeses'.

The leaves can be cooked and eaten like spinach, added to thicken soups, or deep-fried like green wafers.

The flowers and buds can be pickled.

NUTRITIONAL PROFILE

Common mallow is a highly nutritious green, containing (per 100 g of fresh weight) 4.6 g protein, 1.4 g fat and 24 mg vitamin C, as well as vitamin A and caretonoids.

The fats contain important omega-3 and omega-6 fatty acids, which could help to reduce the incidence of chronic diseases such as cancer, diabetes and heart disease.

The leaves also contain health-giving antioxidants and are a good source of dietary fibre.

HERBAL MEDICINE USES

Common mallow was once a 'cure-all' of medieval herbal medicine. It was used to treat many conditions, from stomach ache to problems during childbirth.

In Britain and Ireland, the plant has been used as a laxative, to cleanse the liver, to cure blood poisoning, and to treat urinary problems, rheumatism, heartburn, coughs and cuts.

The mucilaginous roots, were used to make poultices and soothing ointments.

OTHER USES

There are no particular uses for common mallow outside food and medicine, although the pretty flowers can be used for decoration around the home.

CAUTIONS

The seeds may be poisonous if eaten in large quantities (Quattrocchi, 2012).

25

MEADOWSWEET

FILIPENDULA ULMARIA

Meadowsweet is an ancient plant of the British Isles that has lived here at least since the last ice age.

It was famous in medieval Britain for its sweet-smelling, almond-fragranced flowers that were popular for strewing on floors to scent a room.

It later became recognised, like willow, for its salicylic acid content, and was used for many of the same complaints as aspirin today, such as coughs, colds, headaches, sore throats and fevers.

Nicholas Culpeper (c.1653) hailed meadowsweet, or mead sweet, as 'Queen of the Meadows'.

The flower was also known as 'brideswort' and was once used in bridal bouquets in summer months.

Another name for the plant was 'courtship-and matrimony', with the scent of the flowers before and after bruising thought to represent the change before and after marriage. Make of that what you will.

In other traditions, the name 'courtship-and-matrimony' is thought to come from the sweet-smelling flowers contrasting with the sharper, bitter-smelling leaves.

Given its reputation as a flavouring for alcoholic drinks, the ancients praised meadowsweet for its 'power of allaying the furies of drunkenness' (Palaiseul, 1977).

PARTS USED FOR FOOD

Leaves, flowers, roots.

FOOD USES

Meadowsweet was famous as a honey-wine herb. *'Meadwort'*, or *'Medwort'*, was one of fifty ingredients in a drink called 'Save' mentioned by English author Geoffrey Chaucer in *The Knight's Tale* (c.1387).

Nicholas Culpeper (c.1653) also recommended a leaf of meadowsweet in a cup of claret wine to give it a 'fine relish'.

Today, meadowsweet is one of thirty herbs and spices added to the popular Norfolk punch cordial drink, originally made by the monks of Norfolk, England.

All parts of the plant can be added to soups, sauces or stewed fruit for an aromatic flavour.

The bitter roots have been used as a tea substitute along with the leaves and flowers.

NUTRITIONAL PROFILE

Meadowsweet is considered a good example of the old adage: 'let food be your medicine', thanks to its reputation for soothing over-active stomachs and treating coughs and colds.

HERBAL MEDICINE USES

Meadowsweet's most famous claim to medicinal success is as a forerunner of aspirin. It was Felix Hoffman in 1897 who first synthesised the drug salicin from the salicylic acid of mead-owsweet.

The plant has been considered the go-to herb for indigestion, flat-ulence, gastric ulcers, gastric reflux, liver disorders, cystitis, diar-rhoea in children, rheumatism, cellulitis, bladder stones, and oedema.

OTHER USES

Meadowsweet was also used to scour milk churns.

CAUTIONS

Despite its acclaimed success, Foster and Duke (2014) warn that all salicylic-containing plants should be used with caution given that salicylic medicines can thin blood and cause internal bleeding.

26

MUGWORT

ARTEMISIA VULGARIS

Mugwort is one of our commonest weeds, with around 250–300 species growing in northern Europe, including wormwood, south-ernwood and the common mugwort.

As a group of plants, mugworts held an important place in antiquity. They were dedicated to Artemis in Greek mythology, and to her equivalent, Diana – goddess of the moon, women and child-birth - in Roman mythology.

Her temples were places of healing and her sacred herb was often used for curing female-related illnesses.

An ancient story tells of Queen Artemisia, who was sister, consort and successor to Mausolus (c376–353 BC) of Caria in southwest Anatolia. Around 352 BC she built a monument to her husband Halicarnassus, using mugworts (Cleene and Lejeune, 2003).

We don't know for sure whether the common mugwort was the same *Artemisia* of legend, but it's likely to be the same plant known to herbalists in the Middle Ages.

Traditionally, mugwort has been considered to be a female plant, which reflects its mythical origins; another species in the same group, wormwood, is considered to be male.

Common mugwort was known as the *Mater Herbarum*, or mother of herbs, in Europe, with a formidable reputation as a magical plant, a reliable remedy for female complaints, and an effective nerve tonic.

> *Eldest of worts*
> *Thou hast might for three*
> *And against thirty.*
> *For venom availest*
> *For flying vile things,*
> *Mighty gainst loathed ones*
> *That through the land rove.*
> Saxon MS. Herbal (Harleian) *1585*

PARTS USED FOR FOOD

Leaves, stalks, flower buds, flowers.

FOOD USES

Mugwort can be used as an aromatic herb added to soups, stews or stuffing for meat dishes, or infused as a tea. The herb is said to improve digestion and has been used as a stuffing for goose, duck and other fatty meats.

The young stems can be added to salads, and the leaves or shoots can be cooked as a vegetable.

NUTRITIONAL PROFILE

The plant is rich in vitamin C and unsaturated fatty acids.

HERBAL MEDICINE USES

Mugwort is sometimes referred to as the 'women's herb' because it was used to promote menstruation and induce childbirth.

Another common use for the plant was to treat stomach disorders, including stimulating the appetite, easing nausea or curing worms.

OTHER USES

The plant is sometimes used as an ingredient in perfumes and soaps.

It has also been used as an insect repellant.

In Ireland, the leaves were smoked as a substitute for tobacco, which was said to stimulate poor appetites.

CAUTIONS

Mugwort should not be used during pregnancy because it can promote menstruation.

NAVELWORT OR PENNYWORT

UMBILICUS RUPESTRIS

There is a tendency to overlook navelwort in favour of the house-leek (*Sempervivum tectorum*) in folklore and folk medicine.

David Allen and Gabrielle Hatfield (2004) consider the medical uses of both plants – specifically the fleshy leaves – as 'so broadly similar that they must surely have stood in for one another to no small extent'. Yet it is the navelwort that is undoubtedly a native plant of the British Isles, largely found in western parts, and the house-leek that is a 'relic of long-forgotten introductions'.

The house-leek is thought to be a hybrid of a mountain plant of central Europe, which is mostly dependent on propagation by humans.

Let us focus on our humble navelwort, sometimes known as wall pennywort or pennyleaf.

PARTS USED FOR FOOD

Leaves, seeds, stem.

FOOD USES

The succulent leaves make a juicy addition to salads or as a sandwich filling with chives or sorrel. They have a mild flavour when picked in winter or early spring and can be eaten raw.

The leaves, seeds and stems of navelwort can also be candied.

NUTRITIONAL PROFILE

The plant's juice is thought to be diuretic and anti-inflammatory, and may be drunk as a tonic for the liver and spleen.

HERBAL MEDICINE USES

Traditionally, navelwort was used in Britain as a remedy for inflammations, cuts, chilblains and skin infections, and for stones in the body such as kidney stones. The plant's sap has also been used to relieve bee stings.

Its use as a medicinal herb is scattered throughout history. In Irish folk medicine, it was also put to use to treat a wide number of ailments, including jaundice, tuberculosis and skin complaints, as well as for lumps and bumps, headaches, worms, fevers, liver problems, and bladder stones.

OTHER USES

The plant yields a yellow and a red dye.

CAUTIONS

Its safety during pregnancy or when breastfeeding has not been established.

28

OXEYE DAISY

LEUCANTHEMUM VULGARE

A familiar sight in fields, the oxeye daisy is found throughout Britain, Europe and Russia. Where it was introduced to North America, the plant spread so rapidly that North Carolina adopted oxeye daisy as its state flower.

Its former genus name, *Chrysanthemum*, derives from the Greek *chrisos* (golden) and *anthos* (flower). The specific name – oxeye – means 'white flower'.

Today, *Leucanthemum vulgare* is more commonly used: *leucanthemum* meaning 'white', referring to the flowers, and derived from the Greek *leucomo*.

The name 'daisy', in general, comes from *day's eye* because the flower closes at night.

Of course, like most daisies, the oxeye daisy is well known for the children's game of 'She loves me, she loves me not', or simply for being made into 'fairy chains', now more commonly known as 'daisy chains'.

Indeed, in Goethe's Faust, it is the *Sternblume* (star flower, or oxeye daisy) that Margaret asks: *'Er liebt mich – lieb mich nicht.'*

In Bavaria, Germany, there is a similar weather divination using oxeye daisy: *'Schea, shiach ...'* (Good, bad).

PARTS USED FOR FOOD

Leaves, stem, flower buds, flowers.

FOOD USES

Oxeye daisy is a palatable salad vegetable. The petals, stem and leaves can be eaten raw in salads or sandwiches or added to soups and stews.

The plant can be bitter. It is recommended that the youngest specimens are picked and added sparingly to salads or other dishes like omelettes.

The young shoots and buds can be eaten lightly steamed for an aromatic flavour.

The flower heads can also be used for decorating salads and other dishes.

NUTRITIONAL PROFILE

The leaves are thought to be high in vitamins A and C, betacarotene, riboflavin, niacin and potassium, but low in carbohydrates. The petals are also high in betacarotene and niacin.

HERBAL MEDICINE USES

Another name in England for the plant was *'bruise wort'*, because the crushed leaves were applied to heal bruises.

Its abundance across the British Isles led to its use for many ailments including coughs, chills, boils, jaundice, wounds, tuberculosis and sore eyes.

OTHER USES

A specimen of lace made from oxeye daisy was donated by Lady Doneraile to the Economic Botany Collection at the Royal Botanic Gardens, Kew.

CAUTIONS

While oxeye daisy can be eaten as a hiker's snack, it is advised not to eat the yellow centre of the flower as it may cause indigestion.

Consuming large doses of oxeye daisy can cause sickness in some people.

29

PLANTAIN

PLANTAGO SPP.

Greater plantain (*Plantago major*) and ribwort plantain (*Plantago lanceolata*) belong to a big family of plants called Plantaginacea. There are around 200 species in the plant group.

Of these, twenty-five to thirty species have had a medicinal, culinary or other domestic use in our history and culture.

Plantains are a versatile wild edible and herbal remedy. Here, we focus on the greater and ribwort plantains.

Plantain flourishes in different habitats around the world. In America and New Zealand it was called 'Englishman's foot' or 'white man's foot', because it was believed to have followed British settlers as they colonised new land. On my recent teaching tour to the USA, I learned that this is in fact incorrect. Blackseed plantain (*Plantago rugelii*) was a native species in the eastern states long before the settlers got there.

The plantains took advantage of agricultural practice in Britain, Ireland and Europe; pollen samples date back some 3-4,000 years.

Its seeds long served as food, having been found in the stomachs of mummified 'bog people' of fourth century northern Europe.

It is a perennial opportunist, because of its survivalist nature.

Plantain is disliked by gardeners, because it destroys grass with its vigorous rosette of leaves. Ribwort plantain is even less popular with hayfever sufferers, because of its highly irritant pollen.

No doubt plantain is a useful species, but be warned - if the wind changes when you pick it, you could go mad.

PARTS USED FOR FOOD

Leaves, flower buds, seeds.

FOOD USES

Plantain leaves are picked and used as a salad green, vegetable or potherb.

The flower buds have a distinct mushroom taste and are delicious fried in butter.

The seeds can be ground to make flour.

NUTRITIONAL PROFILE

As a wild edible, plantain species are considered highly nutritious, containing vitamins A, B, C and K, fibre, fat, protein, silicon, calcium, sodium, zinc, tannin and mucilage.

The nutty-flavoured seeds are also a good source of protein. But beware, until you get used to them they can be highly laxative!

HERBAL MEDICINE USES

Plantain has been used as a general remedy for many complaints from cuts, sores and bruises to kidney disease, bowel disorders and intestinal worms.

Its primary use in folk medicine has been as a healer of wounds, and it was once valued as a cure for animal bites and stings. I have personally noticed that when I have applied the crushed leaf to a cut, it has acted as a mild analgesic (pain reliever).

As an all-round remedy for major and minor ailments, the many different species of plantain are often interchangeable in herbals.

It was considered a great healer and in particular a vulnerary herb for its ability to prevent external bleeding.

OTHER USES

The seeds were once collected to feed small caged birds.

CAUTIONS

Eating too much plantain may have a laxative effect and could lower blood pressure.

There is little data on the plant's toxicity.

PRIMROSE

PRIMULA VULGARIS

The primrose is one of the first spring flowers you may notice in your garden. In the language of flowers it means 'youth', although in the fickleness of youth the primrose says: 'Maybe I will love you. I cannot say yet' (Cleene and Lejeune, 2003).

The popularity of its bright, yellow blossoms have made the flower scarce in some areas. It has been suggested that its decline is also due to changes in woodland management and the loss of the shaded habitat so favoured by the plant.

In medieval Latin, primrose, or *prima rosa*, meant 'first rose' of the year.

In early literature, there is a lack of clarity between *P. vulgaris* and the common cowslip (*P. veris*). The two plants are often referred to interchangeably, or as one and the same, in folklore and customs.

Even in today's herbals, primroses and cowslips are frequently listed as the same entry, such as in Richard le Strange's *A History of Herbal Plants* (1977), which describes the attributes of cowslips, primroses and auriculas under the general heading 'Primula'.

PARTS USED FOR FOOD

Leaves, flowers.

FOOD USES

The mild, sweet-scented flowers can be eaten raw in vegetable or fruit salads.

Primrose flowers can also be used in conserves, custards, mousses, tarts or other desserts and confections.

The leaves make an alternative salad green and have a spicy taste with a slight anise aroma.

They can be cooked as a vegetable in a pot, added to soup, or mixed with other herbs as a stuffing for meat and poultry.

Both blooms and leaves can be made into syrups and teas.

NUTRITIONAL PROFILE

Primrose leaves contain vitamin C and minerals. The whole plant, particularly the root, contains saponins, glucosides and various other substances.

HERBAL MEDICINE USES

Primrose flowers have enjoyed a reputation for healing wounds for centuries. An ointment made of flowers boiled in lard would be applied to cuts, burns and other skin ailments.

Today, primrose is used in skin preparations for pimples and wrinkles, and is often used in soothing eye washes.

OTHER USES

Primrose is a valuable source of forage to bees in winter and early spring.

CAUTIONS

Some texts advise that *P. vulgaris* should not be used by pregnant women, patients sensitive to aspirin, or those on anti-coagulant drugs such as warfarin.

RED CLOVER

TRIFOLIUM PRATENSE

Red clover is an abundant wild herb. It is plentiful in Ireland,Britain and Europe, where it is planted as an important fodder crop for livestock.

White clover (*Trifolium repens*) is equally common in Ireland and Britain. Its uses in food and medicine are comparable to red clover, but it is red clover which is the focus here.

Gerard referred to *T. pratense* as the 'three-leafed grass' but acknowledged that there were many kinds of clover which he left to be distinguished by 'the curious'.

Dreaming of clover is said to foretell good health and prosperity. The ancients would sometimes depict 'hope' as a small child holding a clover flower.

As a general charm, clovers were also considered to be 'noisome' to witches and to deter them.

PARTS USED FOR FOOD

Leaves, stem, flowers, roots.

FOOD USES

Red clover is an extremely versatile herb. The fresh leaves and flower heads can be added to salads and sandwiches, or added to soups, or boiled.

The dried leaves and flower heads can be sprinkled on dishes such as boiled rice. The fresh or dried flowers make a refreshing herbal tea or country wine.

NUTRITIONAL PROFILE

Red clover is rich in nutrients such as vitamins A, B3, B12, C, E and K, and minerals calcium, magnesium, chromium, iron, manganese, potassium and selenium as well as trace amounts of zinc.

HERBAL MEDICINE USES

Red clover was once used to purify the blood by drinking an infusion of the blossoms in honey. This remedy was also used to soothe a cough. A decoction of the flowers was considered to be sedative.

However, the plant is most famous in medicine for mimicking the effects of the hormone oestrogen and providing a treatment for menopausal symptoms.

OTHER USES

Clovers are important nectar sources for insects, so if you don't fancy eating clover yourself, please keep clover on your lawn for hungry bees.

In Irish folk medicine, red clover leaves were once used as a treatment for bee stings – another reason to invite this flower into your garden.

CAUTIONS

Because of its oestrogenic effects, red clover is not recommended during pregnancy or when breastfeeding.

It may also be harmful to people who have tumours.

Diseased clover can contain toxic alkaloids.

ROSEBAY WILLOWHERB

EPILOBIUM ANGUSTIFOLIUM

Every herb garden should grow rosebay willowherb for a splash of colour and a buzz of bees. The tall, striking plant graced the garden of 16th-century herbalist John Gerard. He wrote in his herbal:

> *A goodly and stately plant having leaves like the greatest willow or osier, garnished with brave flowers of great beautie, consisting of four leaves apiece of an orient purple colour.*

Gerard was the first to record rosebay willowherb as a British species. Since his lifetime, the plant has spread across the country with seemingly single-minded determination, to become a familiar sight along railways and roadsides.

Where woodlands are cleared, buildings fall or fire scorches the earth, rosebay willowherb rises like a phoenix from the ashes.

The rosy-pink flowers bloomed on the sides of Mount Saint Helen three weeks after the volcano erupted. After the Blitz of London in World War II, Lewis Gammett in the 25th July 1944 edition of the *New York Herald Tribune* reported on another invasion of the city:

> There is the brilliant rose-purple plant that Londoners call rose-bay willow herb ... It sweeps across this pockmarked city and turns what might have been scars into flaming beauty.

In England, rosebay willowherb became known as bombweed. It truly is an opportunistic species.

It is attractive to pollinating insects, but can also self-seed and disperse on the wind. This was discovered by German geographer and polymath Matthias Christian Sprengel (1746–1803).

The dead flowers fall off the plant after pollination and the pods open to reveal silky, white, fluffy seed puffs scattered by the wind. The seed puffs are produced in such abundance they can form great clouds on windy days. Collecting the fluffy seed puffs can make a good tinder for fire in winter, but take care not to unintentionally clear more land for the fire-loving herb.

A number of different species of willowherb may be illustrated in early and modern herbals. For example, in Britain, the great hairy willowherb (*E. hirsutum*), with its striking, bell-shaped flowers, grows alongside ponds.

In Ireland, too, the rosebay willowherb (*E. angustifolium*) is a commonplace weed at the verges of roads, railways and on waste ground. It is also occasionally found along mountain trails.

The Irish call it 'blooming sally', which derives from *Salix* – the Latin name for willow. A species of willowherb from New Zealand (*E. brunnescens*) was introduced to Ireland as a garden plant, but has since become a common weed.

In North America, the species most used in ethnobotany are *E.*

angustifolium, E. latifolium and *E. palustre.* It is well known as 'fire-weed' in the States – a name that may have migrated with it from Europe. It has been suggested that it originated from the West Country in England, though Robert Dale Rogers (2014) suggests it derived from the German *Feuerkraut*, named by 16th century Swedish naturalist Conrad Gessner because it flourished on burned ground.

PARTS USED FOR FOOD

Leaves, shoots, stems.

FOOD USES

For centuries in Russia, rosebay willowherb was fermented to make herbal tea, nicknamed 'Ivan Chai' in Britain and Europe. It is also known as 'Kaporie tea'.

It was eventually replaced by the black and green teas from India and China, but is still drunk in some parts of Russia.

The flavour of this fiery-looking plant has been described as mildly sweet, like cucumber or asparagus.

The shoots can be cooked like asparagus or the leaves and stems lightly boiled or steamed like spinach.

NUTRITIONAL PROFILE

Rosebay willowherb has ninety times more vitamin A, and four times more vitamin C, than oranges.

HERBAL MEDICINE USES

Few records exist of the herb's use in folk medicine in Britain, but it was used in Europe and America, especially for skin complaints, whooping cough in children, asthma and stomach disorders.

In modern herbals, its properties are often listed as astringent, antidiarrhoeic, demulcent (soothing and anti-inflammatory), haemostatic (stopping bleeding) and mildly antimicrobial.

OTHER USES

Fireweed is such a good source of nectar that US beekeepers sometimes follow loggers with their hives.

Fireweed honey is said to be light-coloured and finely flavoured.

CAUTIONS

The plant's tannins might aggravate constipation, gastric ulcers, inflammatory conditions and anaemia.

33

SAXIFRAGE

CHRYSOSPLENIUM SPP.

The golden leaves of this moisture-loving plant, and one of its uses in ancient medicine, led to its Latin name, which incorporates the two words *chrysos*, meaning 'gold', and *splen*, meaning 'spleen'.

Despite its attractive appearance, golden saxifrage has not apparently attracted much folklore over the centuries.

PARTS USED FOR FOOD

Leaves.

FOOD USES

Saxifrage is a useful salad leaf, known as *cresson de roche* in the Vosges mountains of eastern France. The leaves are also added to soups.

It is listed as a potherb in some texts and as an emergency food plant in others.

NUTRITIONAL PROFILE

There is little known of its nutritional value.

HERBAL MEDICINE USES

Saxifrage is a species open to research. Few studies have been done on the medicinal properties of this plant, and few records are available of its past use in folk medicine.

OTHER USES

The succulent, golden leaves and stems, fresh or dried, could provide interest in flower arrangements.

CAUTIONS

There is little information about toxicity and side effects.

Make certain that you cook this plant. On one occasion I ate some from a spring and became extremely ill due to water contamination.

There is no clean 'wild water' anymore and I always recommend cooking any plants that grow in or around water.

34

SCURVYGRASS

COCHLEARIA SPP.

The leaves of this wild edible were eaten raw by sailors as a remedy for scurvy, which lent the plant its common name of scurvygrass.

Scurvy is a potentially fatal disease caused by vitamin C deficiency, the onset of which is marked by bleeding gums.

Scurvygrass was well known as a cure for scurvy in the Shetlands. Royal Vickery (1997) recalls a saying:

> *God so ordering it in his wise Providence... seeing the scurvy is a common Disease of the Countrey, they should have the Remedy at hand.*

The uses of each individual species of *Cochlearia* are largely similar and interchangeable, and use was likely made of whichever variety was available to pick. Scurvygrass was without doubt an important plant in the prevention and treatment of a once-prevalent disease.

In the 16th to 18th centuries, in Sussex, England, for instance, many people suffered from the condition; although the connection between the disease and nutritional deficiencies was little understood.

Scurvy afflicted both urban and rural communities at a time when fresh vegetables (certainly available to many in rural areas) were not as popular as meats, fish, pies, cheeses and puddings, and when vegetables were only available seasonally and/or were often overcooked.

Scurvygrass, although unwittingly to those who ate it, provided the much-needed dietary intake of vitamin C. Since citrus fruit became more widely available, scurvygrass has been neglected as a valuable source of this nutrient.

PARTS USED FOR FOOD

Leaves.

FOOD USES

The tender, juicy leaves of several scurvygrass species are edible and may be eaten cooked or raw. The flavour is sweet and slightly salty, with a pungency reminiscent of horseradish or cress.

Scurvygrass makes a crisp salad leaf and can be eaten between bread and butter like watercress.

Traditional recipes suggest mixing the raw salad herb with other clean, sharp tastes such as capers, lemons and oranges, or with oil and vinegar to complement boiled eggs.

NUTRITIONAL PROFILE

As well as being rich in vitamin C, scurvygrass contains the mineral iodine, as well as tannins, glucosides and other substances.

HERBAL MEDICINE USES

To treat scurvy, the bright, green leaves of scurvygrass were traditionally picked in spring after a long winter, when fresh fruit and vegetables were scarce.

The root, too, had many uses in folk medicine: as a diuretic for relieving urinary stones, gout and sciatica, as a bruised poultice for paralytic conditions, and as a syrup for coughs.

OTHER USES

None known.

CAUTIONS

There is little information on the side effects of scurvygrass.

3 5

SEA ASTER

ASTER TRIPOLIUM

The Elizabethans were so enchanted by the blue-purple, star-like flowers found along the seashore, that they invited the sea aster into their gardens.

Its resemblance to daisies earned it the common names 'blue daisy' or 'blue chamomile'.

By 1640 its star had begun to fade with the arrival of Michaelmas daisies from the New World, although the name 'Michaelmas' probably applied both to our native sea aster and the introduced species.

In the language of flowers, sea aster means 'afterthought', which seems fitting for a small salt-marsh plant that appears as little more than a footnote in the great herbals of the past.

PARTS USED FOR FOOD

Leaves, stems, flowers.

FOOD USES

Sea asters were once gathered in pre-industrial Sweden for stews and soups, although they were largely considered to be fodder for livestock and only eaten by people when other crops were scarce.

The fleshy leaves are sometimes collected to make a pickle.

Today the sea aster has been caught up in a tide of interest about wild food plants and the potential for new and exciting commercially-produced crops. The plant has been sold by a small southern-Swedish foraging company to NOMA restaurant in Copenhagen.

NUTRITIONAL PROFILE

Sea aster, like other salt marsh plants, is a good source of protein. This is particularly true of the salty leaves (Joshi and Khot, 2004).

HERBAL MEDICINE USES

Sea aster's use as a medicinal plant has been limited to treating wounds, fluid retention and poisoning.

A root decoction has sometimes been used to treat headaches and toothaches (Eland and Lucas, 2013).

OTHER USES

None known.

CAUTIONS

Studies into the metal uptake from soils in wetland plants have included an analysis of the effects on sea aster.

Shaibur and team (2008) studied arsenic levels in sea aster; they found it to be largely concentrated in the roots and not a concern to the plant's overall toxicity.

36

SEA BEET

BETA VULGARIS SUBSP. MARITIMA

Sea beet is the wild ancestor to common vegetables such as beetroot, swiss chard and spinach beet. We can even thank this rugged coastal plant for the sugar in our cup of tea or coffee, because it was the original to sugar beet too.

The coastal plant belongs to the pigweed (Amaranthaceae) family, and is one of many subspecies of beet (*Beta vulgaris*) that have been hybridised by humans over the past 2,000 years.

While the bright crimson slices of beetroot are more familiar on our plate, sea beet is an ancient food and medicine plant. It has been used since prehistory, but over time it has relinquished its place at the table in favour of its cultivated cousins.

The origin of beet (*Beta*) species is thought to be the Middle East, from whence it spread west to the Mediterranean, and north along the Atlantic coast.

PARTS USED FOR FOOD

Leaves.

FOOD USES

Use as you would Swiss chard, spinach or beetroot greens. It's delicious and needs very little preparation.

NUTRITIONAL PROFILE

Sea beet contains high levels of vitamin C – about 36 mg per 100 g.

The fresh young leaves are high in vitamins K (988 mg per 100 g) and B (302 mcg per 100 g), and nutrients such as calcium (67 mg per 100 g), zinc (845 mcg per 100 g), and iron (almost 3 mg per 100 g).

The plant is a good source of dietary fibre (Sánchez-Mata and Tardío, 2016).

HERBAL MEDICINE USES

Sea beet has a long history of folk use, particularly in the treatment of tumours. A decoction was made from the seed or juice, and other parts of the plant were prepared to treat tumours, leukemia, breast and womb cancers, as well as other cancers such as those of the stomach, prostate, head or spleen.

The leaves and root were once used as an emmenagogue – to induce menstruation.

OTHER USES

Modern research into sea beet has observed its ability to grow in salty soils, which might prove an advantage to crop-growing when better soils are unavailable in famine-stricken countries.

CAUTIONS

As with other plants such as spinach, dock and cultivated chard, excessive use of beets can cause hypocalcemia (a deficiency of calcium in the bloodstream) and anaemia, kidney damage or toxicity because of the plant's oxalate content.

37

SEA PURSLANE

ATRIPLEX PORTULACOIDES

This slow-growing shrub belonging to the goosefoot family is found in salt marshes and on muddy beaches.

It is fairly common along the coast of Britain and Ireland.

PARTS USED FOR FOOD

Leaves, seeds.

FOOD USES

As a seaside plant, sea purslane makes an excellent pickle, much like the more commercially used samphire.

The crunchy, salty leaves make a tasty addition to salads, stir fries and fish dishes.

The plant can be cooked as a vegetable or potherb, or boiled and served in a similar way to French beans.

The seeds are far easier to gather than the leaves, and vast quantities can be collected in a very short time. I use them to make a delicious pesto.

NUTRITIONAL PROFILE

There is little information available on the nutritional content of sea purslane.

HERBAL MEDICINE USES

Sea purslane gained a reputation in folk medicine as a remedy for women's complaints such as menstrual problems and uterine disorders, and for 'hysterical fits'.

However, there are few records of its use and it may have been substituted in favour of more effective plants.

OTHER USES

None known.

CAUTIONS

Research has suggested that sea purslane does not contain toxic levels of heavy metals from coastal soils.

The plant should be thoroughly washed before use.

38

SELFHEAL

PRUNELLA VULGARIS

Selfheal was so called because it was once believed to be one of the best wound herbs that people could safely take to heal themselves.

The ancient doctrine of signatures – a belief that 'like cured like' – ruled that selfheal was a 'styptic' that could staunch the bleeding from cuts. From Pior (1870):

> *... from its corolla seen in profile being shaped like a bill-hook, and, on the doctrine of signatures, supposed to heal wounds from edged tools, the self-heal.*

Selfheal was also known as 'Hercules' wound' because it was said that the hero learned of the plant's healing virtues from Chiron the Centaur.

PARTS USED FOR FOOD

Shoots, leaves, flowers.

The leaves and young shoots of this wild edible are versatile greens that can be eaten raw in salads, added to soups and stews, or used as a potherb. The flavour is similar to romaine lettuce.

The leaves – freshly chopped, dried or powdered – can be soaked in cold water to make a refreshing beverage.

NUTRITIONAL PROFILE

Selfheal contains vitamins A, B, C, K, flavonoids, and rutin.

The plant's high content of antioxidants has been the subject of much recent research.

HERBAL MEDICINE USES

In early medicine, selfheal had a reputation as a wound herb. John Gerard (1597) wrote:

> *It serveth for the same that Bugle doth, and in the world there are not two better wound herbes as hath been often prooved.*

Modern herbalism records selfheal as a topical emollient, astringent and vulnerary herb.

The leaves and stems are said to be antibacterial, astringent, diuretic, hypotensive (reducing blood pressure), efficacious for haematuria (blood in urine), antitumour and a powerful antioxidant.

The flower spikes have also been said to restore the liver, and new research suggests that selfheal does indeed possess hepatoprotective (liver-protecting) properties. The plant is also said to be a tonic for the gallbladder in that it stimulates and promotes healing in that organ.

OTHER USES

The cylindrical, spiked flowers make attractive additions to flower arrangements, either fresh or dried.

CAUTIONS

Allergic reactions to selfheal have been reported (Gardner et al., 2013).

39

SOWTHISTLE

SONCHUS SPP.

The hollow stem of sowthistle yields a white, milky juice which is said to have been given to sows to increase the flow of their milk (Wyse Jackson, 2013).

The Latin name of the genus 'sowthistle' is *Sonchus* meaning 'hollow'.

There are many species of *Sonchus* (*Sonchus* spp.) – all are edible, and most are indistinguishable in appearance – but the two most commonly used for food and medicine are smooth sowthistle (*S. oleraceus*) and prickly sowthistle (*S. asper*).

Sowthistles are sometimes confused with dandelions, because of the appearance of their bright yellow flowers and green spiny leaves.

They may also be mistaken for milkthistle due to their creamy sap, but sowthistles are unrelated to true milkthistle (*Silybum marianum*).

The sowthistle has a complicated relationship with humans. It has flourished in the path of human progress to become a common weed and wild edible.

Along the way, some people have become devoted to its tender young leaves and juicy stem, while others have found its bitterness less agreeable.

PARTS USED FOR FOOD

Leaves, buds, stem, flowers.

FOOD USES

Sowthistle has been used as a salad and potherb since the days of our early ancestors. The younger plants are mildly bitter and quite succulent; older plants are very bitter and tough.

The leaves and stems of prickly and smooth sowthistle can be cooked like vegetables, added to stir fries and stews.

The juicy stem should be milked before cooking because the juice can turn parts of the plant brown.

NUTRITIONAL PROFILE

Sowthistle has four times as many antioxidant compounds as red wine, and twelve times as many as black tea; it is rich in essential fatty acids and minerals and nutrients like zinc, manganese, copper, iron, calcium and fibre (Kallas, 2010).

Its traditional use as an ingredient in spring dishes eaten for health and vitality is supported by its high content of vitamins A, B, C and K. 100 g fresh weight of various sowthistles contains between 30 and 60 mg of vitamin C, and smooth sow thistle has been shown to contain up to 800 mg of vitamin A. (Sánchez-Mata and Tardío, 2016; Kuhnlein, 1991; Wiersema and León, 2013)

HERBAL MEDICINE USES

The medicinal virtues of smooth sowthistle (*S. oleraceus*) were believed to be similar to dandelion (*Taraxacum officinale*).

The creamy milk in the stem was used as a cure for warts.

Sowthistle was also used as a herbal remedy to hasten childbirth, to treat skin and eye problems, and to freshen foul breath.

OTHER USES

The fluffy seeds were once used to stuff pillows and mattresses.

CAUTIONS

Smooth sowthistle is said to be more toxic than other species of sowthistle; the white latex produced by the plant is mildly poisonous to lambs and horses, and the roots are said to induce abortion.

40

SORREL

RUMEX ACETOSA

The common sorrel is a plant of many names. One of its most charming is 'cuckoo's meat', because of an old belief that it cleared the cuckoo's throat and restored the bird's iconic, bubbling cackle.

There is such a variety of sorrels, and such a cornucopia of local names, that you may be forgiven for some confusion over which species is which in different herbals.

Its most familiar name is from the French *surele*, rooted in *sur* and meaning 'sour'.

Other local names, such as sooricks, sour grabs and sour leeks, also stem from the herb's sour taste.

Common sorrel was in popular use in England at the time of King Henry VIII, in and around the 16th century.

Along with many 'ordinary' herbs, Nicholas Culpeper felt the English sorrel growing around and about needed no description. He assigned it to the dominion of Venus, the planet and goddess of love in Roman mythology, with little explanation.

As a medicinal and garden herb, common sorrel has been used since the ancient days of Greece's Dioscorides and Rome's Pliny the Elder, in the 1st century AD.

Its tendency to appear as one of the first plants in spring meant it was once a highly valued edible green.

Its arrow-shaped leaves were a familiar sight in medieval vegetable gardens across Europe until the 1700s, and it has since become a common wild herb in North America where it was introduced as a salad green.

PARTS USED FOR FOOD

Leaves, stalks.

FOOD USES

Common sorrel is distinctly sour, which makes it a tasty addition to salads. It can also be used to make a sharp side dish or condiment to accompany red meat, for instance with roasts or stews.

Children once snacked on the sour-tasting leaves and stems of common sorrel.

The wild edible was once known as 'the poor man's herb' because of its ready availability to foragers.

NUTRITIONAL PROFILE

Common sorrel contains high amounts of vitamin C – 75 g of chopped fresh sorrel leaves provide around half of the daily requirement for an adult. It also contains beta carotene, which is converted to vitamin A by the body (*Herbalpedia*, 2016).

HERBAL MEDICINE USES

Sorrel was believed to be a 'cooling' herb and helpful for swellings and inflammatory conditions.

The plant was used to treat fevers, skin tumours, jaundice, and internal ulcers.

Sorrel also had a number of common uses such as treating wounds, sores, bruises, boils and chickenpox.

OTHER USES

Sorrel contains potassium bioxalate, otherwise known as 'sorrel salt'. This was once sold as 'essential salt of lemons' and used to bleach straw or remove stains and rust marks from linen.

CAUTIONS

Common sorrel is thought to contain oxalate crystals and is best not consumed in large quantities.

Like other docks, sorrel can trigger hayfever or aggravate asthma in some people.

41

STINGING NETTLE

URTICA DIOICA

Nettle's long relationship with human culture has led to a number of different applications. Some stranger than others.

It is said that nettle drives frogs from beehives, although few modern beekeepers complain about frogs in their hives.

In addition, nettle oil was once burnt in lamps, and the plant was hung in kitchens as a fly deterrent – though apparently it was not particularly effective.

Mashed nettles make a cheap and nutritious poultry feed, being particularly good for young turkeys.

It is said that cattle who are fed nettle produce better milk, and chickens who eat nettle lay more and stronger eggs.

The plant makes a rich black compost which is great for gardeners. In Dublin, gardeners are said to use nettles to turn green gooseberries a reddish colour by layering the fruit with nettles in a tub.

In France paper was made from nettle fibres.

A principle use of nettle was for making cloth – a practice which dates back to the Bronze Age.

In Hans Christian Andersen's tale The Wild Swans (1850), a young princess weaves eleven shirts made from nettle to lift a spell cast on swan brothers.

Nettles were cultivated in Scotland, Denmark and Norway to make fishnets, coarse sailcloth and fine linens. After flax was introduced, nettle cloth, or 'scotchcloth', was still woven for household use from the 16th to 19th centuries.

The Scottish poet Thomas Campbell (1837) wrote about nettle:

> In Scotland, I have eaten nettles, I have slept in nettle sheets, and I have dined off a nettle table-cloth. The young and tender nettle is an excellent pot-herb, and the stalks of the old nettle are as good as flax for making cloth.

The green of nettle was associated with St Patrick's Day in Scotland and Ireland where it was popularly used for dye and cloth.

Nettle is described as having a long association with indigenous cultures in North America, particularly in British Columbia, Alaska and the Aleutians, where it was an important source of stem fibre for cordage (cords and ropes, such as for ship's rigging).

Until fairly recently, in parts of northern Europe, nettle was still cultivated for making cloth. In the First World War, Germany reportedly used large quantities of nettle – around 2½ million kg - to make military clothing. The resultant German uniforms were 85% nettle fibre. In the Second World War, nettle was collected by schoolchildren to use as a dye, and nettle dye was used to camouflage uniforms in Britain.

A study by Eser and Onal (2015) found that nettle leaf extract was a potent natural colouring for dying wool and cotton fabrics, with the potential to be an important agent for today's textile industry.

PARTS USED FOR FOOD

Leaves, flowers, stems, shoots.

FOOD USES

The shoots and leaves were traditionally picked as a spring tonic. Nettle 'pudding' or 'porridge' was eaten in parts of Britain as a 'pick-me-up after the winter' (Hatfield, 2008).

Modern research has revealed that nettle contains vitamin C and iron, which explains its use as a spring vegetable.

Cooking the plant, even briefly, destroys the stinging hairs and makes nettle safe to eat.

Today, nettle is also a popular herbal tea.

NUTRITIONAL PROFILE

Nettle is packed full of vitamins A and C, and some B vitamins. Fresh nettles contain (per 100 g) 670 mg potassium, 590 mg calcium, 18 mcg chromium, 270 mcg copper, 86 mg magnesium, and 4.4 mg iron (Kress, 2018).

HERBAL MEDICINE USES

Nettle was considered to be a 'warming' herb because of its stinging hairs. This made it a popular treatment for rheumatism and other conditions such as sciatica that benefit from rubbing a stinging plant on the body to stimulate circulation.

Roman soldiers famously rubbed their bodies with nettle to promote good circulation and to stay warm.

OTHER USES

Nettle was often woven into cloth for household use – a practice dating back to the Bronze Age.

CAUTIONS

Nettle's most unpleasant effect is itching and swelling caused by its stinging hairs, which can be more severe in some people.

42

THREE-CORNERED LEEK

ALLIUM TRIQUETRUM

You might be forgiven for thinking at first glance that the three-cornered leek is a grass of some kind, but as soon as you crush the leaves, or any part of the plant, its garlicky smell is revealed.

It is called 'three-cornered' because the flower stem when cross-sectioned appears triangular, while the leaves also have a ridge down them resembling the keel of a ship. The drooping flowers have been described as a 'white bluebell'.

Found throughout England, Wales and Ireland, but rare in Scotland, *A. triquetrum* was first cultivated in England in 1759, though according to Geoffrey Grigson (1955), in Cornwall at the time you could be fined for allowing it to grow due to the plant being highly invasive.

PARTS USED FOR FOOD

Leaves, flowers.

FOOD USES

The young, tender leaves can be added to salads in place of spring onion for their milder, oniony flavour, and the flowers added as a garnish.

The leaves can also be fried, boiled and served with cream sauce, or used in leek soup.

NUTRITIONAL PROFILE

There is little data available on the nutrient value of three-cornered leek.

TRADITIONAL MEDICINE USES

While *Alliums* like garlic are often added to the diet for their beneficial effect on blood cholesterol and for use as a digestive tonic, three-cornered leek is rarely mentioned in past or present herbalism.

OTHER USES

The plant's juice is said to repel moles and insects.

CAUTIONS

The plant may cause contact dermatitis.

43

VIOLET

VIOLA SPP.

There are around 400 species of violet found in the world, many of which are economically important.

With so many species to distinguish between, and so many popular names to identify them, in literature there is often much confusion around the description of 'violet'.

A possible origin of the name is the Greek mythological character *Io, lover* of Zeus, or Jupiter. The king of the gods changed Io into a cow to hide her from his jealous wife Hera, or Juno, and then created violets as food for the cow. For this reason, the violet is sometimes known as *Jupiterbloem,* or 'Jupiter's flower' in Flemish.

Geoffrey Grigson suggests that what really pulled the violet out of obscurity was its scent. He writes:

> Scent suggested sex, so the violet was a flower of Aphrodite and also of her son Priapus, the deity of gardens and generation ... A flower so deeply and finely scented must also have its virtues in physic.

PARTS USED FOR FOOD

Leaves, flowers.

FOOD USES

Violet flowers can be crystallised and used as edible decorations. The flowers also make a pretty garnish sprinkled over salads, omelettes, cakes and desserts.

Sweet violet flowers were used by celebrity Marcus Wareing at the Chelsea Flower Show to garnish his gin and tonic. If you fancy something simpler, violet tea is easily made by pouring hot water over the petals or flower heads, and is just as likely to impress at tea parties.

The chopped leaves can be added to salads and soups, or dipped in batter and fried as an appetiser. The leaves also make a tasty sandwich in bread and butter.

NUTRITIONAL PROFILE

Violet leaves are high in vitamin C as well as containing vitamin A and various minerals and saponins. Research suggests the plant also has significant antioxidant activity.

HERBAL MEDICINE USES

Violet root is used in remedies for coughs, colds, bronchitis and sore throats because of its expectorant and stimulating effects. The root is also used to make eyewashes and mouthwashes, and to treat thrush.

Violet leaf tea can also be drunk for coughs. The leaves are considered to be antiseptic and can be taken internally as a tea, or externally as a compress.

OTHER USES

V. odorata is one of the most economically important species of violet. It is grown commercially in southern France for the production of essential oils in the manufacture of perfume, flavouring and cosmetics.

Around 100 g of flowers are used to produce 31 g of essential oil of violet by a process of macerating the petals in hot fat (Uphof, 1959). About 1000 g of violet leaves are used to produce 400 g of violet absolute. The absolute and essential oils have a wide variety of uses in perfumes and cosmetics for hair and skin.

CAUTIONS

Several sources suggest that overuse of violet can be harmful, thus it is a herb to use in moderation (Uphof, 1959). Side effects may include vomiting (Karalliedde et al., 2008).

Best to avoid using violet during pregnancy and when breast-feeding (Karalliedde et al., 2008).

44

WHITE DEAD NETTLE

LAMIUM ALBUM

The white dead nettle is not related to stinging nettle (*Urtica dioica*), but the plant does give its Latin name to the dead nettle family, the *Lamiaceae*. The genus name *Lamium* is from the Greek *laimos*, meaning 'throat', and reflects the form of the flower.

Although native to England, Wales and Scotland, its distribution in Dublin found it around Norman settlements, leading some to believe they brought it with them from France.

The 'dead' in its common name refers to the fact that the plant lacks the sting of nettle. Lord Avebury wrote:

> It cannot be doubted that the true nettle is protected by its power of stinging, and that being so, it is scarcely less clear that the Dead Nettle must be protected by its likeness to the other.

Another common name, 'archangel', refers to the plant's habit of flowering around the feast day of St Michael the Archangel on 8 May. It has also been called 'adam-and-eve-in-the-bower' in recognition of its likeness to two human figures when turned upside down; look for the black and gold stamens (Adam and Eve) lying side by side beneath the white upper lip of the flower.

PARTS USED FOR FOOD

Leaves, flowers, stems.

FOOD USES

The tender leaves and stem tips can be eaten raw, boiled and eaten as a potherb or vegetable, and the leaves chopped and added to omelettes. The leaves can also be treated like spinach.

Serve the young flowering tops lightly steamed, mixed with spring onions and dressed with butter.

For sweet treats or garnish, the flowers can be candied. A wine is still made from the flowers in Yorkshire, England.

NUTRITIONAL PROFILE

White dead nettle leaves contain about 6.5 g of protein, 76 mg of vitamin C and an incredible 644 mcg vitamin A per 100 g of fresh weight.

The greens are similarly nutritious and contain other constituents such as 76 mg calcium, 34 mg phosphorus, 411 mg potassium, 23 mg magnesium, and 3.4 mg iron per 100 g of fresh plant material.

HERBAL MEDICINE USES

As a women's herb, white dead nettle has been used to relieve heavy, painful periods and for leucorrhoea, a white or yellow discharge of vaginal mucous.

In Irish folk medicine, white dead nettle, along with red dead nettle (*L. purpureum*), was mainly used as a treatment for skin complaints.

In parts of England, white dead nettle was a remedy for skin problems and bleeding cuts.

A lotion made from the flowering tops was applied to piles and varicose veins.

OTHER USES

White dead nettle flowers are a helpful crop for bees, while Pliny believed the plant discouraged snakes from entering the garden.

CAUTIONS

The white dead nettle is generally considered a safe plant to use in food and medicine. There are no known contraindications during pregnancy, when breastfeeding, or when taking prescribed medications.

45

WILD ANGELICA

ANGELICA SYLVESTRIS

The popular group called 'angelica' is named after the Greek *angelos*, which means 'a messenger'.

In Christian myth, angelica revealed itself as a cure for the plague in an archangel's dream, and for centuries it was placed above all other healing herbs. The English herbalist and botanist John Parkinson (1629) wrote:

> ...*it is so goode an herbe that there is no part thereof but is of much use.*

There are around thirty species of angelica, but it is garden angelica (*Angelica archangelica*) that is most mentioned in old and new herbal texts. The wild angelica, with its tall, furrowed, purplish stalks and delicate umbels of flowers that 'seem to have been dipped in claret' (Grigson, 1955), is an almost forgotten plant.

Its species name *Sylvestris* means 'wild, of or from woods or forests', yet it is angelic by association to *A. archangelica* and has acquired many archangel names through time.

Wild angelica is a native British species, but by the days of the great herbalists, such as Parkinson, Gerard, and Culpeper, garden angelica had made its way across Europe (originating from Syria according to some authorities) to cooler, northern climates, and had reached as far as Lapland and Iceland. It's thought that garden angelica was introduced to Britain around 1568 and fast became the apothecary's favourite herb. To unearth the story of wild angelica, we must look at the story of garden angelica without losing sight of the woodland flower.

PARTS USED FOR FOOD

Stalk, leaves, flowers, root.

FOOD USES

A traditional use for angelica – both wild and garden– is as a candied decoration for cakes and sweets. Garden angelica is more often used, because the leaf stalks and stems are not as tough and bitter as the wild variety.

The shoots, stalks or stems are boiled till soft, then peeled, and the fleshy pulp is crystallised by soaking in sugar syrup and baking in the oven.

Wild angelica is almost as versatile in the kitchen as garden angelica, and it can be used as a substitute for garden angelica in most recipes for sweet and savoury dishes.

Boil the young leaves and stems to eat as a vegetable or chop the leaves and add to stewed fruit like rhubarb. The sweet-tasting roots are also edible, and the aromatic seeds can be used as a culinary spice.

NUTRITIONAL PROFILE

There is little information on the nutritional properties of wild angelica.

HERBAL MEDICINE USES

Wild angelica is often recorded in herbals as a poorer substitute for garden angelica. Like garden angelica, it may be used for many complaints, from lung and chest diseases to rheumatism and corns. However, garden angelica is often the preferred plant of choice.

There are specifically documented uses for wild angelica in Irish folk medicine. For example, chewing the roots of the plant before breakfast was said to cure heart palpitations and promote urination.

Irish records also document wild angelica as a treatment for epilepsy, and to treat hydrophobia (a fear of water that was a symptom particularly associated with rabies in humans).

It may also be helpful as a medicinal food. The plant can be useful for minor stomach upsets and indigestion thanks to its antispasmodic and anti-inflammatory actions.

OTHER USES

Young children once used the plant's hollow stems as 'pea shooters'.

CAUTIONS

Like all species of angelica, wild angelica contains phototoxic compounds called furanocoumarins that may cause sensitivity to the sun.

Wild angelica juice may also cause a rash or skin inflammation in some individuals.

46

WILD GARLIC OR RAMSONS

ALLIUM URSINUM

Wild garlic is a plant of shady, damp woodlands, fields and hedgerows. Its clusters of tiny white flowers and bright green leaves form a carpet beneath the trees in some places, while in other areas they are quite scarce.

The English naturalist William Turner (1510–1568) in 1548 knew the plant as ramsey, bucrammes (buck rammes) and rammes, and several places in England share its name, such as Ramsbottom (meaning 'Ramson valley') in Lancashire and Ramsey (meaning 'Ramson island') in Essex and Huntingdonshire.

The name ramsons was a metaphor for bitterness in Irish folklore. There was a saying in County Donegal: 'As bitter as wild garlic'.

PARTS USED FOR FOOD

Leaves, shoots, flowers, seed, bulbs.

FOOD USES

Wild garlic can be used in the same way as its domesticated cousin, or true garlic. Finely chop or bruise the plant to use raw in salads and sandwiches, or boil and mix with other vegetables to make soups, stews, sauces and side dishes.

The leaves can be used as an alternative to garlic to make wild garlic salt, wild garlic butter, wild garlic bread and so on.

NUTRITIONAL PROFILE

Wild garlic leaves per 100 g contain 45 mg of vitamin C and almost 5 mg of beta carotene.

The bulbs per 100 g have 16 mg of vitamin C and over 2 mg of protein.

HERBAL MEDICINE USES

As with domesticated garlic, wild garlic can be eaten to help fight off coughs and colds.

Traditionally, wild garlic was a widely used medicinal herb used to treat a range of ailments including toothache, sore eyes, warts, measles, mumps and rheumatism.

Modern research suggests that, like garlic, eating wild garlic may help to reduce blood cholesterol and lower blood pressure.

OTHER USES

The garlic-smelling leaves were used in Scotland to repel midges.

CAUTIONS

Some people are allergic to plants related to garlic. Reported side effects from taking wild garlic range from bad breath and stomach upsets to allergic reactions (Wiersema and León, 2013).

Overindulgence in the herb can also cause flatulence and heartburn (Duke, 2002).

The plant has been known to thin blood and therefore is not suitable for people taking blood-thinning medication without first seeking medical advice (Wiersema and León, 2013).

47

WOOD AVENS

GEUM URBANUM

Wood avens, or herb bennet, is a woodland member of the rose family (*Rosaceae*). Curiously, the plant's Latin name *urbanum* means 'city dweller', which is where this wild flower of hedges and woods was also once found.

The generic name *Geum* derives from the Greek *geno,* meaning an agreeable fragrance. This is a reference to the slightly aromatic leaves and spicy-smelling roots.

PARTS USED FOR FOOD

Leaves, roots.

FOOD USES

The roots and rhizomes are aromatic with the spicy scent of cloves. Add for flavour to soups, broths, stews, sauces, fruit pies and stewed fruit. Combine the root with orange peel and add to wine or other mulled drinks, gin and beer.

Alternatively, boil in milk to make an Indian-style chai tea. The leaves can also be infused to make a mildly spicy cordial.

The dried plant can be used as seasoning and the young leaves added to salads.

NUTRITIONAL PROFILE

There is little data on the nutritional value of wood avens. However, the aromatic roots do contain eugenol – the main chemical constituent of clove oil, the essential oil distilled from cloves (*Syzygium aromaticum*).

TRADITIONAL MEDICINE USES

The roots and rhizomes have been used in traditional herbal medicine for treating various problems: gastrointestinal disorders, such as diarrhoea, dyspepsia, constipation, indigestion, stomach upsets and appetite loss; oral disease, such as throat and mouth infections; skin complaints, such as chilblains and haemorrhoids.

OTHER USES

Traditionally, the herb's aromatic roots were dried and used as a flea repellent or placed among clothes to deter moths.

CAUTIONS

Because of its high tannin content, some texts recommend that the herb is not used in large quantities.

48

YARROW

ACHILLEA MILLEFOLIUM

Yarrow's botanical name *Achillea millefolium* derives from its prolific foliage, meaning 'milfoil' or 'thousand leaf'.

It has earned its place in our folk history as a long-standing medicinal and magical herb, from the days of the ancient Greeks and Romans through the time of the Anglo-Saxons up until the present day.

PARTS USED FOR FOOD

Leaves, flowers.

FOOD USES

Yarrow's peppery foliage and bitter leaves and flowers bring an aromatic flavour to salads.

The leaves can be used in almost any dish as a vegetable, added to soups and sauces, or simply boiled and simmered in butter as a side dish.

The flowering tops can be sprinkled on salads and other dishes as a condiment or decoration.

NUTRITIONAL PROFILE

None known at this time.

HERBAL MEDICINE USES

In herbal medicine, yarrow was valued as an astringent herb for scratches, cuts, wounds and sores. It was also called 'soldiers' woundwort' and 'staunch grass' due to its ability to staunch bleeding. The ancient Romans new it as *Herba militaris*.

Yarrow tea is thought to help purify blood and cleanse skin.

OTHER USES

Dried yarrow leaves were once used as a substitute for tobacco.

CAUTIONS

Yarrow may cause skin irritation in some people.

It is best avoided during pregnancy and when breastfeeding.

PLEASE LEAVE A REVIEW

Much as I'd like to, I don't have the financial muscle of a London or New York publisher. I can't take out full page ads in newspapers or put posters on the underground or in bus stops. (Sound of violins).

As an independent author, I don't receive funding from government, corporations or charities etc. So I am indebted to my loyal readers (like you) for spreading the word about my work.

If you've enjoyed this book, I would be grateful if you could spend five minutes leaving a review (it can be as short as you like) on the book's Amazon's page.

Honest reviews of my books help bring them to the attention of other readers.

Thank you very much.

ABOUT THE AUTHOR

Robin Harford is a plant-based forager, ethnobotanical researcher and wild food educator. He has published over 50 foraging guide books.

He established his wild food foraging school in 2008, and his foraging courses were recently voted #1 in the country by BBC Countryfile.

Robin is the creator of eatweeds.co.uk, which is listed in The Times Top 50 websites for food and drink.

He has travelled extensively documenting and recording the traditional and local uses of wild food plants in indigenous cultures, and his work has taken him to Africa, India, SE Asia, Europe and the USA.

Robin regularly appears on national and local radio and television. He has been recommended in BBC Good Food magazine, Sainsbury's magazine as well as in The Guardian, The Times, The Independent, The Daily Telegraph etc.

facebook.com/foragingcourses
twitter.com/robinharford
instagram.com/robinjharford

MORE BOOKS FROM ROBIN HARFORD

Over the years I have published over fifty foraging guidebooks. They aren't all on Amazon or in other bookstores, so if you'd like to see my back catalogue, please visit:

eatweeds.co.uk/foraging-guide-books

BIBLIOGRAPHY

Allen, D. E. & Hatfield, G. (2004) *Medicinal Plants in Folk Tradition: An Ethnobotany of Britain & Ireland*. Portland, OR: Timber Press.

Al-Snafi, A. (2018) *Chemical Constituents and Medical Importance of Galium Aparine-a Review*. [Online]

Andersen, H. C. (1850) *The Wild Swans and Other Tales from Andersen*. London: Blackie & Son.

Anon (2016) *Herbalpedia*.

Antal, D. (2010) Medicinal Plants with Antioxidant Properties from Banat Region (romania): A Rich Pool for the Discovery of Multi-Target Phytochemicals Active in Free-Radical Related Disorders. *Analele Universitatii din Oradea, Fascicula Biologie*. TOM XVII.

Baker, M. L. (2008) *Discovering the Folklore of Plants*. Oxford: Shire.

Barros, L. et al. (2010) Leaves, Flowers, Immature Fruits and Leafy Flowered Stems of Malva sylvestris: A Comparative Study of the

Nutraceutical Potential and Composition. *Food and Chemical Toxicology*. [Online] 48 (6), 1466–1472.

Bartram, T. (1998) *Bartram's Encyclopedia of Herbal Medicine*. New York: Marlowe.

Bennet, S. (1991) *Food from Forests*. Dehra Dun, India: Indian Council of Forestry Research and Education.

Bertoli, A. et al. (2004) Volatile Constituents of Different Parts (roots, Stems and Leaves) of Smyrnium olusatrum L. *Flavour and Fragrance Journal*. [Online] 19522–525.

Biancardi, E. et al. (2012) *Beta maritima: The Origin of Beets*. [Online]. New York: Springer-Verlag.

Campbell, T. (1837) *Letters from the South.* , 2 vols. London: H. Colburn.

Candolle, A. de (1959) *Origin of Cultivated Plants*. New York: Hafner Pub. Co.

Carvalho, I. S. et al. (2011) Fatty Acids Profile of Selected Artemisia spp. *LWT - Food Science and Technology*. [Online] 44 (1), 293–298.

Cleene, M. D. & Lejeune, M. C. (2003) *Compendium of Symbolic and Ritual Plants in Europe: Vol I Trees & Shrubs/Vol II Herbs*. 01 edition. Ghent: mens & cultuur uitgevers n.v.

Couplan, F. (1998) *The Encyclopedia of Edible Plants of North America*. New Canaan, Conn.: Keats Pub.

Culpeper, N. (1841) *Culpeper's Complete Herbal*. London: J.S. Pratt.

Duke, J. A. (2002) *Handbook of Medicinal Herbs*. 2nd ed. Boca Raton, FL: CRC Press.

Eland, S. C. & Lucas, G. (2013) *Plant Biographies*.

Elias, T. S. & Dykeman, P. A. (2009) *Edible Wild Plants: A North American Field Guide to Over 200 Natural Foods*. New York: Sterling.

Eser, F. & Onal, A. (2015) Dyeing of Wool and Cotton with Extract of the Nettle (Urtica dioica L.) Leaves. *Journal of Natural Fibers*. [Online] 12 (3), 222–231.

Facciola, S. (1998) *Cornucopia II: A Source Book of Edible Plants*. Vista, CA: Kampong Publications.

Fernald, M. L. et al. (1996) *Edible Wild Plants of Eastern North America*. New York: Dover Publications.

Fogg, G. E. (1950) Sinapis Arvensis L. *Journal of Ecology*. [Online] 38 (2), 415–429.

Folkard, R. (1884) *Plant Lore, Legends, and Lyrics*. London: Sampson Low, Marston, Searle, and Rivington.

Foster, S. & Duke, J. A. (2014) *Peterson Field Guide to Medicinal Plants and Herbs of Eastern and Central North America*. Peterson field guides. Third edition. Boston: Houghton Mifflin Harcourt.

Gardner, Z. E. et al. (eds.) (2013) *Botanical Safety Handbook*. 2nd ed. Boca Raton: American Herbal Products Association, CRC Press.

Gasparetto, J. C. et al. (2012) Ethnobotanical and Scientific Aspects of Malva sylvestris L. *Journal of Pharmacy and Pharmacology*. [Online] 64 (2), 172–189.

Gray, B. (2011) *The Boreal Herbal: Wild Food and Medicine Plants of the North*. Whitehorse, Yukon: Aroma Borealis Press.

Grieve, M. (1931) *A Modern Herbal. The Medicinal, Culinary, Cosmetic and Economic Properties, Cultivation and Folk-Lore of Herbs, Grasses, Fungi, Shrubs & Trees*. London: Jonathan Cape.

Grigson, G. (1955) *The Englishman's Flora*. London: Phoenix House.

Grzeszczuk, M. et al. (2016) Biological Value of Various Edible Flower Species. *Acta scientiarum Polonorum. Hortorum cultus = Ogrodnictwo*. 15.

Guarrera, P. M. & Savo, V. (2016) Wild Food Plants Used in Traditional Vegetable Mixtures in Italy. *Journal of Ethnopharmacology*. [Online] 185202–234.

Guil, J. L. et al. (1997) Nutritional and Toxic Factors in Selected Wild Edible Plants. *Plant Foods for Human Nutrition (Dordrecht, Netherlands)*. [Online] 51 (2), 99–107.

Haines, A. (2010) *Ancestral Plants: A Primitive Skills Guide to Important Edible, Medicinal, and Useful Plants*. Southwest Harbor, Me.: Anaskimin.

Hatfield, G. (2004) *Encyclopedia of Folk Medicine: Old World and New World Traditions*. Santa Barbara, Calif: ABC-CLIO.

Hatfield, G. (2008) *Hatfield's Herbal: The Secret History of British Plants*. London: Penguin.

Irving, M. (2009) *The Forager Handbook*. London: Ebury.

Joshi, A. & S. Khot, S. (2004a) *Edible Succulent Halophytes as Good Source of Proteins for Restoration of Salt-Affected Soils*.

Joshi, A. & S. Khot, S. (2004b) *Edible Succulent Halophytes as Good Source of Proteins for Restoration of Salt-Affected Soils*.

Kallas, J. (2010) *Edible Wild Plants: Wild Foods from Dirt to Plate*. Wild food adventure series. 1st ed. Layton, Utah: Gibbs Smith.

Karalliedde, L. et al. (2008) *Traditional Herbal Medicines*. London: Hammersmith Press.

Kershaw, L. (2017) *Edible & Medicinal Plants of the Rockies*.

Klooss, S. et al. (2016) Charred Root Tubers of Lesser Celandine (

Ficaria verna Huds.) in Plant Macro Remain Assemblages from Northern, Central and Western Europe. *Quaternary International.* [Online] 40425–42.

Komarov, V. L. (1970) *Flora of the U.S.S.R. Volume VII: Ranales and Rhoeadales.* Vol. 7. Smithsonian Institution.

Kreicbergs, V. (2011) *Biologically Active Compounds in Roasted Coffee.* 6.

Kress, H. (2018) *Practical Herbs 1.* London: Aeon Books.

Kuhnlein, H. V. (1991) *Traditional Plant Foods of Canadian Indigenous Peoples.* Food and nutrition in history and anthropology v. 8. Philadelphia: Gordon and Breach.

Kunkel, G. (1984) *Plants for Human Consumption: An Annotated Checklist of the Edible Phanerogams and Ferns.* Koenigstein: Koeltz Scientific Books.

Le Strange, R. (1977) *A History of Herbal Plants.* London: Angus & Robertson.

Lentini, F. & Venza, F. (2007) Wild Food Plants of Popular Use in Sicily. *Journal of Ethnobiology and Ethnomedicine.* [Online] 315.

Lightfoot, J. (1792) Google-Books-ID: C_cnAAAAYAAJ. *Flora Scotica, Or, A Systematic Arrangement, in the Linnæan Method, of the Native Plants of Scotland and the Hebrides.* J. Dickson, G. Mudie, J. Elder.

Lim, T. K. (2013) *Edible Medicinal and Non-Medicinal Plants: Volume 5, Fruits.* [Online]. Springer Netherlands. [online].

Łuczaj, Ł. et al. (2012) Wild Food Plant Use in 21st Century Europe: The Disappearance of Old Traditions and the Search for New Cuisines Involving Wild Edibles. *Acta Societatis Botanicorum Poloniae.* [Online] 81 (4), 359–370.

Łuczaj, Ł. & Pieroni, A. (2016) 'Nutritional Ethnobotany in Europe: From Emergency Foods to Healthy Folk Cuisines and Contemporary Foraging Trends', in María de Cortes Sánchez-Mata & Javier Tardío (eds.) *Mediterranean Wild Edible Plants*. [Online]. New York, NY: Springer New York. pp. 33–56.

Mabey, R. (1977) *Plants with a Purpose: A Guide to the Everyday Uses of Wild Plants*. London: Collins.

Mabey, R. & Blamey, M. (1972) *Food for Free*. London: Collins.

Mac Coitir, N. & Langrishe, G. (2015) *Ireland's Wild Plants: Myths, Legends and Folklore*.

MacNicol, M. (1972) *Flower Cookery: The Art of Cooking with Flowers*. New York: Collier Books.

Maggi, F. et al. (2012) A Forgotten Vegetable (Smyrnium olusatrum L., Apiaceae) as a Rich Source of Isofuranodiene. *Food Chemistry*. [Online] 135 (4), 2852–2862.

Mahajan, V. et al. (n.d.) Ethnobotanical Inventory on Medicinal Plants of North Western Himalayas. *Journal of Krishi Vigyan*. 6.

Mears, R. & Hillman, G. (2008) *Wild Food*. Hodder & Stoughton.

Mills, S. Y. & Bone, K. (eds.) (2005) *The Essential Guide to Herbal Safety*. St. Louis, Mo: Elsevier Churchill Livingstone.

Montaut, Sabine & Bleeker, R. (2011) Cardamine sp. – A Review on Its Chemical and Biological Profiles. *Chemistry & biodiversity*. [Online] 8955–975.

Montaut, S. & Bleeker, R. S. (2011) Cardamine Sp. - a Review on Its Chemical and Biological Profiles. *Chemistry & biodiversity*. [Online] 8 (6), 955–975.

National Institute of Science Communication (New Delhi, I. (2000) *The Useful Plants of India*. New Delhi: National Institute of

Science Communication, Council of Scientific & Industrial Research.

Negi, P. S. & Subramani, S. P. (2015) *Wild Edible Plant Genetic Resources for Sustainable Food Security and Livelihood of Kinnaur District, Himachal Pradesh, India.* 6657–668.

Newall, C. A. et al. (1996) *Herbal Medicines: A Guide for Health-Care Professionals.* London: Pharmaceutical Press.

Nyerges, C. (2014) *Guide to Wild Foods and Useful Plants.* Chicago: Chicago Review Press.

Pachauri, T. et al. (2012) '*Analysis of Nutrient Content of Underutilized Grain: Chenopodium Album*', in [Online]. pp. 93–96.

Palaiseul, J. (1977) *Grandmother's Secrets.* Penguin Books Ltd.

Parkinson, J. & Switzer, A. (1629) *Paradisi in Sole Paradisus Terrestris.* London: Humfrey Lownes and Robert Young.

Pedersen, M. (2010) *Nutritional Herbology: A Reference Guide to Herbs.*

Pieroni, A. (ed.) (2014) *Ethnobotany and Biocultural Diversities in the Balkans: Perspectives on Sustainable Rural Development and Reconciliation.* New York: Springer.

Prior, R. (1863) *On the Popular Names of British Plants: Being an Explanation of the Origin and Meaning of the Names of Our Indigenous and Most Commonly Cultivated Species (1870).* London: Williams and Norgate.

Pulsipher, L. M. & Kermath, B. (n.d.) *Food Plants in the Americas: A Survey of the Domesticated, Cultivated, and Wild Plants Used for Human Food in North, Central and South America and the Caribbean.*

Qasem, J. R. (2015) Prospects of Wild Medicinal and Industrial

Plants of Saline Habitats in the Jordan Valley. *Pakistan Journal of Botany*. 47551–570.

Quattrocchi, U. (2012) *World Dictionary of Medicinal and Poisonous Plants: Common Names, Scientific Names, Eponyms, Synonyms, and Etymology*. Boca Raton, Fla: CRC.

Quave, C. L. & Pieroni, A. (2015) A Reservoir of Ethnobotanical Knowledge Informs Resilient Food Security and Health Strategies in the Balkans. *Nature Plants*. [Online] 1 (2), 14021.

Redzić, S. (2010) Use of Wild and Semi-Wild Edible Plants in Nutrition and Survival of People in 1430 Days of Siege of Sarajevo During the War in Bosnia and Herzegovina (1992-1995). *Collegium Antropologicum*. 34 (2), 551–570.

Rogers, R. (2014b) Fireweed – a Treasured Medicine of the Boreal Forest. *Discovery Phytomedicine*. [Online] 1 (1), 10.

Rohde, E. S. (1969) *A Garden of Herbs*. Rev. and enl. ed. New York: Dover Publications.

Runyon, L. (2007) *The Essential Wild Food Survival Guide*. Shiloh, NJ: Wild Food Company.

Sánchez-Mata, M. de C. & Tardío, J. (eds.) (2016) *Mediterranean Wild Edible Plants: Ethnobotany and Food Composition Tables*. New York: Springer-Verlag.

Sárosi, Sz. & Bernáth, J. (2008) The Antioxidant Properties of Prunella vulgaris L. *Acta Alimentaria*. [Online] 37 (2), 293–300.

Schofield, J. J. (1995) *Discovering Wild Plants: Alaska, Western Canada, the Northwest*. Anchorage: Alaska Northwest Books.

Shaibur, M. R. et al. (2008) Critical Toxicity Level of Arsenic and Elemental Composition of Arsenic-Induced Chlorosis in Hydroponic Sorghum. *Water, Air, and Soil Pollution.* [Online] 191 (1–4), 279–292.

Simkova, K. & Polesny, Z. (2015) Ethnobotanical Review of Wild Edible Plants Used in the Czech Republic. *Journal of Applied Botany and Food Quality.* [Online] 8849–67.

Small, E. (2006) *Culinary Herbs.* 2nd ed. Ottawa: NRC Research Press.

Sousa, A. I. et al. (2008) Heavy Metal Accumulation in Halimione portulacoides: Intra- and Extra-Cellular Metal Binding Sites. *Chemosphere.* [Online] 70 (5), 850–857.

Sturtevant, E. L. (1972) *Sturtevant's Edible Plants of the World.* New York: Dover Publications.

Svanberg, I. (2012) The Use of Wild Plants as Food in Pre-Industrial Sweden. *Acta Societatis Botanicorum Poloniae.* [Online] 81317–327.

Szewczyk, K. et al. (2016) Polyphenols from Impatiens (Balsaminaceae) and Their Antioxidant and Antimicrobial Activities. *Industrial Crops and Products.* [Online] 86262–272.

Tabaraki, R. & Ghadiri, F. (2013) In Vitro Antioxidant Activities of Aqueous and Methanolic Extracts of Smyrnium cordifolium Boiss and Sinapis arvensis L. *International Food Research Journal.* 202111–2115.

Tanaka, Y. & Nguyen Van Ke (2007) *Edible Wild Plants of Vietnam: The Bountiful Garden.* Bangkok: Orchid Press.

Thayer, S. (2010) *Nature's Garden: A Guide to Identifying, Harvesting, and Preparing Edible Wild Plants.* Birchwood, WI: Forager's Harvest.

Thayer, S. (2006) *The Forager's Harvest: A Guide to Identifying,*

Harvesting, and Preparing Edible Wild Plants. Ogema, WI: Forager's Harvest.

Tilford, G. L. (1997) *Edible and Medicinal Plants of the West.* Missoula, Mont: Mountain Press Pub.

Turner, N. J. et al. (2011) Edible and Tended Wild Plants, Traditional Ecological Knowledge and Agroecology. *Critical Reviews in Plant Sciences.*

Uphof, J. C. Th. (1959) *Dictionary of Economic Plants.* New York: H R Engelmann.

Vaughan, J. & Geissler, C. (2009) *The New Oxford Book of Food Plants.* 2 edition. OUP Oxford.

Vickery, R. (1997) *A Dictionary of Plant-Lore.* Oxford paperback reference. Oxford; New York: Oxford University Press.

Waley, A. & Bai, J. (1919) *A Hundred and Seventy Chinese Poems,.* New York: A.A. Knopf.

Watts, D. (2007) *Dictionary of Plant Lore.* Amsterdam: Elsevier.

Wiersema, J. H. & León, B. (2013) *World Economic Plants: A Standard Reference.* 2nd ed. Boca Raton, Fla.: CRC Press.

Williams, C. J. (2010) *Medicinal Plants in Australia. Volume 1, Volume 1,.*

Wyse Jackson, P. (2013) *Ireland's Generous Nature. The Past and Present Uses of Wild Plants in Ireland.* St. Louis, MO: Missouri Botanical Garden Press.

Yaniv, Z. et al. (1991) Differences in Fatty Acid Composition of Oils of Wild Cruciferae Seed. *Phytochemistry.* [Online] 30 (3), 841–843.

Made in the USA
Columbia, SC
30 October 2023

25158953R00100